The Golden Shovel Anthology

# The Golden Shovel Anthology

---

## NEW POEMS HONORING
## GWENDOLYN BROOKS

*Edited by Peter Kahn, Ravi Shankar, and Patricia Smith*
*With a Foreword by Terrance Hayes*

The University of Arkansas Press
Fayetteville
2017

# Contents

## Boy Breaking Glass

## Jessie Mitchell's Mother

## Kitchenette Building

## The Last Quatrain of the Ballad of Emmett Till

**The Second Sermon on the Warpland**

**The Sermon on the Warpland**

**A Song in the Front Yard**

**A Sunset of the City**

**Throwing Out the Flowers**

**To An Old Black Woman, Homeless, and Indistinct**

**To Be In Love**

**To Black Women**

**To the Young Who Want to Die**

**Truth**

**The Vacant Lot**

**We Real Cool**

# Foreword

This project is first and foremost a tribute to Gwendolyn Brooks. Because where do poems come from if not other poems? Where do forms come from if not other forms? So when Peter Kahn brought up the idea an anthology, I may have said something like, "Go for it: Honor Ms. Brooks." Yes, I did write a poem using her "We Real Cool," as the spine, but otherwise, I have done little more than admire Kahn's tireless work to make this anthology come into being. Peter Kahn is the kind of reader of poetry, teacher of poetry, and poet who makes the world easier for other readers, teachers, and poets. Along the way he enlisted the help of the brilliant poets, Patricia Smith and Ravi Shankar, and talked scores of poets into writing their own Golden Shovel poems. I didn't doubt for a moment that he'd produce the marvels awaiting you. The work here, like my own poem, is a way of maintaining, or making material, a link to one of our great poets. (I could just about end this foreword with that.)

When my son was five and my daughter eight, I decided they should each memorize a poem. I gave my daughter a copy of "Luck" by Langston Hughes and my son a copy of "We Real Cool" and had them write the poems out and then recite them to me every day until they had them memorized. As I write this, it sounds a bit like some weird style of parental abuse. I've had time to consider where the idea originated: at the funeral of my father's mother a month beforehand. She was a woman of few words.

Remember Brooks's poem "a song in the front yard"? The speaker has stayed in the front yard all her life, but wants to "peek at the back where it's rough and untended and hungry." My father's mother was a "backyard woman." He was her only child, born when she was fourteen under conditions she never shared. She kept a switchblade folded between her breasts; her hair was a wild plumage as gray as her effusive cigarette smoke before she died of lung cancer. She was the kind of woman Brooks would have depicted in a poem. Sometimes I think of my father's mother when I read "The Mother," or "A Bronzeville Mother Loiters in Mississippi. Meanwhile, A Mississippi Mother Burns Bacon," or "Jessie Mitchell's Mother," or Sadie "[scraping] life with a fine toothed comb," even Winnie Mandela, "the resolving fiction" who "sometimes would like to be a little girl again."

Bear with me. I'm only thinking of Gwendolyn Brooks's myriad portraits of women on my way to the postfuneral scene at the home of one of my father's cousins. When Gwendolyn Brooks died in the winter of 2000, she did not receive, at least beyond Chicago and poetry, a worthy send-off. It should have been a day of national mourning. I don't know about you, but I have been, since her passing, returning to her work again and again with the feeling not enough has been made of it or her. She was the first black writer to receive the Pulitzer Prize for Literature. She was also poet laureate of Illinois from 1969 to 2000, 29th Consultant in Poetry to the Library of Congress, and recipient of the National Book Foundation's Medal for Distinguished Contributions to American Letters. She was a poetry advocate, a poetry patron, a poetry champion. Perhaps we can never say enough about Brooks. Certainly, poets like Elizabeth Alexander, Haki Madhubuti, and anyone graced by Brooks's friendship, teaching, and presence continue to celebrate her. Still there have never been enough tributes, enough parades, enough Association of Writers and Writing Programs panels, enough statues and memorials.

The house, when my father's mother passed, was full of people who were strangers to me. My father is technically my stepfather. His mother never approved of his marriage to my mother when I was four. The sum total of my conversations with her wouldn't fill a page. But that's probably true of everyone she spoke with, maybe even her son. She died a mystery. No one shared stories and recollections as they had when, just a few years before, her sister died. And with no consoling stories to tell about the deceased, they turned inevitably to Bible verses and prayer. I've forgotten which verses were shared, but at some point someone pushed a three- or four-year-old boy into the center of the living room. We were spellbound as he recited the 23rd Psalm from memory with two big clear eyes set in a big freshly barbered head. Then he recited Psalm 24, and then, maybe Psalm 25. It seemed he could have gone on reciting verses by heart all night. When he was done, there was an explosion of applause. A blinding, radiant pride issued from his father's face. Mildly appalled, I said to myself, "Damn, you can fill a kid's head with just about anything." Then mildly awestruck, I said to myself, "Damn, you can fill a kid's head with just about anything!" I decided it should be poems for my kids.

"To some people / Love is given, / To others / Only heaven." "Luck" is just the sort of poem, you'd want a precocious, unchurched eight year old to memorize. My daughter had Hughes's twenty-four words down in ink and mind within a day or two. I knew "We Real Cool" would be a challenge for my five-year-old son. Not simply because of his age, but because of the poem's complexity. It straddles praise and elegy, defiance ("We sing sin.") and acquiescence ("We die soon."). What kind of subliminal impression might it make on my boy? We sat together many nights saying the poem together. Sometimes we put it in the air like a revelry song. It was Hortense Spillers who suggested the very subjects of the poem could deliver the poem as a "drinking/revelry song." Picture seven men so young the slightly older men still call them boys reciting Brooks's poem to each other at the Golden Shovel Pool Hall. Surely it could happen. If you can imagine young black men reciting Common or Kanye or Chief Keef, you can imagine them in a late 1950s South Side Chicago universe reciting Brooks.

We were a dynamic doo-wop duo, my five-year-old and I, practicing Brooks's exquisite twenty-four words at various speeds and volumes. One night, even as I began digging for my own words, Brooks kept playing in my head. I decided to string the whole poem down the page and write into it. It was no more than an exercise. Brooks's poem—her insistent "we" returned me to the pool halls I visited with my father in the seventies. He would have still been in his midtwenties those years. A gold tooth, a pool stick with a green jewel in the handle, a pack of menthol cigarettes. I never saw him drink; I never saw him saddle up to a woman who wasn't my mother. Over the next nights I wrote several more poems using "We Real Cool" as the scaffolding, but only two made it into *Lighthead*, my fourth book. One is a kind of narrative response to Brooks, the other a kind of lyric experiment. I haven't tried the exercise again. I hope what's clear in this foreword is the "Golden Shovel" form belongs to no one so much as Ms. Brooks. Peter Kahn, a citizen of Brooks's Chicago understands as much. My thanks to Gwendolyn Brooks, my thanks to Peter Kahn, Ravi Shankar, Patricia Smith, and each of the poets here.

Terrance Hayes

# Acknowledgments

The editors would like to show our appreciation for the following people who provided extra time, support, and inspiration during this five-year journey: Terrance Hayes; Quraysh Ali Lansana; Kwame Dawes; Afaa Michael Weaver; Steve Young, Don Share, and the Poetry Foundation; Robert Polito; Alice Quinn, Brett Fletcher Laur, Charif Shanahan, and Laurin Macios of the Poetry Society of America; Bianca Stone; Vaughan Fielder; Krista Franklin; Blake Morrison; Goldsmiths-University of London; Becky Swain; Jacob Sam-La Rose; Lisa Mead; Ruth Harrison; John Hodgson; Susannah Herbert; Malika Booker and Malika's Kitchen; David Gilmer; Grace Fondow; Frances Levine; Roger Robinson; Nick Makoha; Sarah Gerton; Frederick Courtright; Tim Seibles; Cynthia Walls and Nora Blakely of the Brooks Estate; Young Chicago Authors; Billy Lombardo and Polyphony High School; the Rogelberg family; Herb, Bonnie, and Lara Kahn; Oak Park/River Forest High School; Steve Gevinson; Mark Doty; Julie Sheehan; Adrian Matejka; A. Van Jordan; Gail Carson Levine; Baron Wormser; Bill Patrick; the MFA program at Fairfield University; Robert Pinsky, Duy Doan, and the Favorite Poem Project; Sandra Beasley; Zachary Clark of 826DC; Lisa Wagner and the Guild Literary Complex; Natasha Trethewey; Richard Blanco; Douglas A. Blackmon; Wesley Rothman; Julie Batten; Rajni Shankar-Brown; Rajee Shankar; Rahini Shankar; Xu Xi; Forrest Gander; Cole Swensen; Jericho Brown; Tina Cane; Thompson Webb; Tom Hazuka; Rand Richards Cooper; Priya Sarukkai Chabria; Brian Turner; Tina Chang; David Carlin; Terri Witek; Jessica Wilkinson; Francesca Rendle-Short; Michelle Aung Thin; Adam Nash; Ken Chen of the Asian American Writers Workshop; Lee Briccetti and Stephen Motika of Poets House; Nicole Sealey, Alison Meyers, and the Cave Canem Foundation; our editors and the terrific staff at the University of Arkansas Press—David Scott Cunningham, Melissa King, and Brian King; and, our amazingly invaluable associate editor, Maura Snell.

David Baker's "Stolen Sonnet" first appeared in *Tin House* (17:1). Used by permission of the author.

Ellen Bass, "Morning ( a twisted shovel)." From *Like a Beggar*. Copyright © 2014 by Ellen Bass. Reprinted with the permission of the Permissions Company, Inc. on behalf of Copper Canyon Press, www.coppercanyonpress.org.

Dexter L. Booth's poem "Neo-Afronaut Anthem" first appeared in *Southeast Review: Raising Our Voices, Claiming Our Words Social Justice Issue* (online). December 2014. Used by permission of the author.

Gwendolyn Brooks's "A Sunset of the City," "kitchenette building," "Boy Breaking Glass," "a song in the front yard," and "The Bean Eaters," all reprinted by consent of Brooks Permissions.

Melisa Cahnmann-Taylor's "Frijolero Ex-Pats" is used by permission of Whitepoint Press LLC.

Curtis Crisler's "On the other side of *that* window" will appear in his forthcoming collection. Used by permission of the author.

Teri Cross Davis's "One Night Stand" is from *Haint* Copyright 2016 by Teri Cross Davis. Reprinted by permission of Gival Press.

Kendra DeColo's "Las Night on Earth We Go to Wendy's" was originally published in *Thieves in the Afterlife* (Saturnalia Books, 2014). Used by permission of Saturnalia Books.

Alison Hawthorne Deming, "Cartoon." Copyright by Alison Hawthorne Deming, from *Stairway to Heaven* by Alison Hawthorne Deming. Used by permission of Penguin Books, an imprint of Penguin Publishing Group, a division of Penguin Random House LLC.

LaTasha N. Nevada Diggs's "Cling" first appeared in *TwERK* (Belladonna* Collaborative, 2013).

Rita Dove's "From the Sidelines" © 2015 by Rita Dove.

Camille Dungy's "Because it looked hotter that way" first appeared in the Academy of American Poets "Poem-A-Day." Used by permission of the author.

Helen Frost, "Softer Sounds." Copyright © 2017 by Helen Frost. Reprinted by permission of Curtis Brown, Ltd.

Reginald Gibbons, "A Neighborhood in Chicago." Copyright 2016 by Reginald Gibbons, from *Last Lake*, by Reginald Gibbons, by permission of University of Chicago Press.

Sandra M. Gilbert's poem "The Fava Bean-Eaters" first appeared in *Prairie Schooner*. Used by permission of the author.

Nikki Grimes, "Storm." Copyright © 2017 by Nikki Grimes.. Reprinted by permission of Curtis Brown, Ltd.

Aracelis Girmay, "After." From *The Black Maria*. Copyright © 2016 by Aracelis Girmay. Reprinted with the permission of the Permissions Company, Inc. on behalf of BOA Editions Ltd., www.boaeditions.org.

Joy Harjo's "An American Sunrise" © Joy Harjo-Sapulpa.

francine j. harris, "The Lot, Vacant Then" first appeared in *Bat City Review.*

Terrance Hayes, "The Golden Shovel." From *Lighthead* by Terrance Hayes, copyright © 2010 by Terrance Hayes. Used by permission of Penguin Books, an imprint of Penguin Publishing Group, a division of Penguin Random House LLC.

Major Jackson, "Stand Your Ground." From *Roll Deep Poems* by Major Jackson. Copyright @ 2105 by Major Jackson. Used by permission of W. W. Norton & Company, Inc.

Gail Carson Levine, "Maud and Sadie." Copyright © 2017 by Gail Carson Levine. Reprinted by permission of Curtis Brown, Ltd.

Nick Makoha's "The Shepherd . . ." is included in his forthcoming collection, *The Second Republic.* Used by permission of the author.

Jamaal May, "The Names of Leaves in War." From *A Brief History of Hostility.* Copyright © 2016 by Jamaal May. Reprinted with the permission of the Permissions Company, Inc., on behalf of the author and Alice James Books, www.alicejamesbooks.org.

Gail Mazur's "Believe That Even in My Deliberateness I Was Not Deliberate" was first published in *New Ohio Review.* Published in *Forbidden City* by Gail Mazur, University of Chicago, 2016. Used by permission of the author.

Patricia McCarthy's poem, "Childless Woman" first appeared in her collection *Shot Silks* from Waterloo Press, UK in 2016. Used by permission of the author.

Colleen McElroy's "Throwing Stones at the All White Pool" appears in *Blood Memory* (University of Pittsburgh Press). Used by permission of the author.

Blake Morrison's "The Road to Wales" was first published in a slightly different form in *Shingle Street* (Chatto & Windus), 2015. Used with permission of the author.

Andrew Motion's "Conjunction" was first was first published in *Peace Talks* (Faber, London, 2015). Used with permission of the author.

John O'Connor's "Immigrant" will appear in a chapbook called *Rooting* from Finishing Line Press. Used by permission of the author.

Elise Paschen's poem "Division Street" first appeared in the Academy of American Poets "Poem-A-Day." "Division Street" will be published in Elise Paschen's book, *The Nightlife* (Red Hen Press, 2017). Used by permission of the author.

Rachel Richardson's "A Halo for Her Invisible Hair" appears as "Vigil" in *Hundred-Year Wave.* Copyright © 2016 by Rachel Richardson. Reprinted with the permission of the Permissions Company, Inc., on behalf of Carnegie Mellon University Press, www.cmu.edu/universitypress.

Roger Robinson's "Brixton Revo 2011" was published in the book *The Butterfly Hotel* by Roger Robinson (Peepal Tree Press). Used with permission of Peepal Tree Press.

Evie Shockley's "song in the backyard" first appeared in the Academy of American Poets "Poem-A-Day." Used by permission of the author.

Myra Sklarew "Money, Mississippi 1955" will be included in her collection of poems, *Sing, Little Collar Button*. Used by permission of the author.

Patricia Smith's article, included in the introduction of this anthology, "Gwendolyn Brooks in the Mecca," first appeared in *Poetry* magazine (Originally Published: April 2, 2012.) Reprinted by permission of the author.

Debris Stevenson's "i. Cecil Park—High as the Swings" and "ii. Dutch Pot Dancing" are included in her collection, *Pigeon Party* from Flipped Eye Ltd. Used with permission of Flipped Eye Ltd.

Stephanie Strickland's poem, "In a Red Hat" appears in two books: *The Body Obsolete* and *New & Selected Poems*. Used by permission of the author.

Dan Sullivan's poem "There Are Mornings" was published in his book *The Blue Line Home* (EM Press). Used with permission of EM Press.

Terese Svoboda's poem "Bird Boy" appeared in *When The Next Big War Blows Down the Valley: Selected and New Poems* published by Anhinga Press, 2015. Used with permission of the author.

Mariahadessa Ekere Tallie's "Gap-Toothed Woman" first appeared in *Hysteria #5*. Used by permission of the author.

Jean Valentine's "Poem with Endwords by Reginald Shephard" appears in her book, *Shirt in Heaven* (Copper Canyon Press, 2015). Used with permission of the author.

Jeanann Verlee's "Careful the Blood" first appeared in *Uncommon Core: Contemporary Poems for Learning and Living*, Red Beard Press. "Careful the Blood" by Jeanann Verlee also appears in her book, *Said the Manic to the Muse*, Write Bloody Publishing. Used with permission of the author.

# Introduction

It was the beginning of my third year as a high-school English teacher at Oak Park/ River Forest High School in 1996. My department head called me into her office and told me she wanted me to host a day at the National Council for Teachers of English annual convention that was being held in Chicago that November. It meant I would have to miss a day of teaching, which hadn't yet happened in my career for any reason, and I wasn't keen to break my streak. The thought of sub plans alone really stressed me out. I told her as much and she said, "You'll be hosting Gwendolyn Brooks for the day." I put in for a substitute teacher later that afternoon.

Spending a day with Ms. Brooks was certainly unforgettable and well worth the nasty sub note I received when I returned to school. Ms. Brooks was wonderfully gracious, kind, and brilliant. She took some time to get to know me and to introduce herself to everyone we encountered (as if we didn't know who she was). A highlight of the day was hearing her explain her rationale for ending all but one line of "We Real Cool" on the word "we." She talked about wanting to emphasize the responsibility of the larger community. I later went on to use "We Real Cool" to teach thousands of students about enjambment while giddily recounting her explanation.

Fourteen years later, I was accepted to study with Terrance Hayes at the Provincetown Arts Center. In preparation, I picked up his most recent book at the time, *Lighthead*, and quickly pored over it. When I reached the poem, "The Golden Shovel," I noticed Terrance's use of enjambment, which like in Ms. Brooks's "We Real Cool," focused on the word "we." The poem had an epigraph: "After Gwendolyn Brooks." After a re-read, I proudly felt I had solved a puzzle: "We Real Cool," in its entirety, worked its way down the right margin of Terrance's poem, imbedded into a stunning new creation. That summer, with Terrance's permission, I wrote a series of my own Golden Shovel poems, playing around with the form a bit. I took a line from a poem or song and ran it down the right margin, as Terrance did, as well as down the left margin in a second poem. I found a level of confidence in borrowing something I loved and getting to utilize it in a creation of my own. I suspected the same would be the case with my students.

Every year I look for prompts that will be accessible, and challenging, to a wide range of students with varying feelings toward poetry (usually intimidation is the most common one). Thus, the fall after working with Terrance, I decided to teach the Golden Shovel form to sophomores (about 850 of them in total), and some of the writing produced was magnificent. I found that the most-reluctant, least-confident students often had success utilizing the form, along with the confident ones. With this form, a synergy seems to occur that is invigorating and helps knock down apprehension and any vestiges of writer's block. Some of my students "borrowed" lines from Ms. Brooks to run down the right margin of their new creations. To draw students in, though, I also allowed them to use "striking lines" from songs they liked. I received Shovels based on songs from Tupac Shakur, Taylor Swift, Bob Dylan, Kanye West, Adele, Nicki Minaj, Lady Gaga, Rihanna, Jay Z, Lil Wayne, and Beyoncé among others. Students were really excited to share what they wrote, and some of the work was the strongest I had seen from them. Along the way, I had a "light bulb moment" and conceived of the idea of an anthology utilizing the Golden Shovel form that would include work from students and teachers, "up-and-comers" and "masters" of the craft of poetry. I figured it would even the playing field a bit by having everyone write using a brand-new form and would be a way for unknown and lesser-known writers to appear beside writers they had studied in school or read on their own.

I approached Terrance for his blessing to create such an anthology. Humble as always, he said that as long as the focus was on Ms. Brooks and the form, and not on him, he was fine with it. That summer at the Southampton Writers' Conference, Julie Sheehan (the program director) recommended approaching Ravi Shankar as a coeditor, and he soon came on board. I then reached out to poets who had worked with my students over the years, such as Patricia Smith, Roger Robinson, Quraysh Ali Lansana, A. Van Jordan, and Kwame Dawes, who all agreed to give it a shot. Patricia—who in 1995 had been the first poet I ever brought to work with my students—is my favorite poet to use in the classroom. I nervously approached her to be the third coeditor and was ecstatic when she agreed. I enlisted the support of Steve Young and Don Share at the Poetry Foundation to gain access to some of my favorite poets, and Ravi, Patricia, and I were on our way. Now, four years after the initial concept, we have an anthology that both introduces a new form and celebrates the legacy of Gwendolyn Brooks. It is with great pride, and with great appreciation for the generous contributions from so many terrific writers, that we introduce *The Golden Shovel Anthology: New Poems Honoring Gwendolyn Brooks.*

Along with Ravi and Patricia, my hope is that the anthology's accessible form and wonderful range of examples will make it a perfect book for helping educators to get their students to approach poetry with an open mind. We envision it being utilized in high-school and college classrooms around the world as well as in homes and libraries by a variety of readers. We are especially excited to help bring a focus on Ms. Brooks as we celebrate her centenary and revisit her powerful poetic legacy.

Peter Kahn

## II.

Celebrated poet T. S. Eliot once wrote that a poet's mind is "a receptacle for seizing and storing up numberless feelings, phrases, images, which remain there until all the particles which can unite to form a new compound are present together," and indeed the history of poetry can be seen through the evolution of formal structures. From the mnemonic and aural devices contained in the ancient Indian *vedas* and Greek epics, to the *formes fixes* of Medieval Europe that gave us *ballades* and *rondeaus*, and then later, sonnets, sestinas, and villanelles, poetry has always been preoccupied with finding that perfect marriage of form and content, those verbal structures that might best support the musicality of perception. So when there is the inception of an original form, one that forms one of the new compounds that Eliot evokes, it is a reason to celebrate.

The Golden Shovel has all the characteristics to be one of the quintessential twenty-first-century forms, one that will last well beyond its moment of inception to take its place in the history of poetic prosody. It's one of the few forms that work both horizontally and vertically, a form that can be seen as a kind of verbal sudoku. It demands an acrostic and cerebral engagement, and—as with more famous and long-established poetic strictures like the aforementioned sonnet, the pantoum derived from Malay fishing songs, or Afaa Michael Weaver's "bop" form based on the blues—it offers the paradoxical freedom of working within a clear formal constraint. The Golden Shovel offers us the pleasure of the encoded secret, of cracking open a fortune cookie at the end of a delicious meal; the last word of each line reaches outside of itself into another text, but if you don't know that, no biggie. You can still engage with the poem as you normally would.

When Peter Kahn approached me about helping to edit this collection, my first instinct was to test it out for myself. And so I took a line from Gwendolyn Brooks and laid it out on the page, each word on its own line, and then I wrote my own Golden Shovel pushing toward those end words. And voilà! A magical transformation occurred. I found myself traveling in directions I didn't expect, and unlike when I have written a sestina, it was a feeling born of pure delight and not the masochistic grinding of trying to repeat the same words over and over again. Having written one, I found I couldn't stop writing them.

The Golden Shovel I've chosen to include in this anthology, "The Narcissist Breaks Up," is based on Ms. Brooks's poem "The Sundays of the Satin-Legs Smith".

My own poem begins:

> Severe narcissistic personality disorder is what **he**
> tells her when he is about to break up with her. **Looks**
>
> victimized by his own flaws, tragically submerging **into**
> shallow pools of self-pitying, trying his best to hold **his**
>
> breath underwater & using the sounds as a **mirror.**

You can see how the last word of each of my lines encodes a line from the middle of Ms. Brooks's own poem, and in its entirety, my poem, when read vertically with the last word of each line, embeds this excerpt from "The Sundays of Satin-Legs Smith."

> He looks into his mirror, loves himself—
> The neat curve here; the angularity
> That is appropriate at just its place;
> The technique of a variegated grace.

The pleasure is in writing a poem of my own construction but referring directly back to another poem. You don't need to know that the poem is a Golden Shovel to engage with its content, but if you do, there's an added layer of meaning and allusion.

I was so smitten with this elegant form that Terrance Hayes had created that I brought it to my college classes and found that my students loved the form as well. And over the last few years, I've taught this form to everyone from senior citizens in a retirement home to third graders who made their Golden Shovels using poster boards, glue sticks, and words from sentences cut out of magazines. Each time, I've found a similar burst of pleasure, that revelatory moment of *aha!*; and I also found an added benefit, which was that the kind of close attention to language that using this form entailed made the students better readers and more observant to the specific language they were using. In some ways, having them write Golden Shovels was one of the best ways I could ever imagine of teaching them the crucial practice of "close reading."

This anthology collects together a wonderful array of poems from some of the world's best poets, all of whom who have written Golden Shovels of their own. And that this book honors Gwendolyn Brooks, whose centenary we are celebrating, is an added bonus as Ms. Brooks was a literary Jackie Robinson, the first black author to win the Pulitzer Prize and to serve as Consultant in Poetry to the Library of

Congress, the progenitor of the position of national Poet Laureate. In some very real ways, she opened the door for many poets who came after her. As another United States Poet Laureate, Rita Dove, has written, "Gwendolyn Brooks was among the few who gave me the courage to insist on my own story. And though I never dreamed of following in her footsteps as far as the Pulitzer Prize, her shining example opened up new possibilities for me and generations of younger artists."

We would like to pay homage to Ms. Brooks's legacy and to introduce the form of the Golden Shovel to a wide readership. There is a particularly modern penchant for marrying the old and new, interfacing on the page with our sources of inspiration and so "telescoping" back through the canon in the course of a single poem. We live in a culture and an era that values collage and sampling, cross-fertilizing, riffing, and remixing. The Golden Shovel is an inherently collaborative effort, a dialogue, a response. For all these reasons, the form has taken off. The torch has been lit! We hope that you will find as much light and inspiration in reading these poems as we have in bringing them to you.

Ravi Shankar

## III.

At first glance, she couldn't even strain toward remarkable. In Chicago, there were legions of colored ladies who looked, moved, sounded just like her. Peppering the street-corner markets, they listened intently to the melons, gathered collard leaves into ragged bundles, shooshed flies away from browning bananas. In the hot middle of some Tuesday, they rode the clacking "L" train, squinting at posted maps during the entire trip, terrified at the thought of missing Pulaski or Garfield. They wore stockings two shades too drooped, the sturdy kind that latched to girdles, although the thick hose always seemed to be wound down to a fat roll just beneath their knees. Their eyes were shutting down, gradually dimming everything the sun did, and they pushed Coke-bottle specs up on their noses with wrinkled forefingers while they glared knowingly at you, fast gal, full as you are with the world.

They were the aunties, the m'dears, the ladies who pressed heads, those sweet whatever-their-names down the street from the Baptist church. They were the warm, insistent presence, a lack of electric. Once you focused and realized they were there—standing in front of and behind you in some line, chortling loud and off-key during Sunday service—there was a comfort about them. Just how they kept being everywhere.

On that blustery February day Gwendolyn Brooks, looking like so many colored ladies of a certain age, of a certain dusted stature, seemed a very small part of the chaos surrounding her. Blues Etc., one of Chi's most storied music haunts, smelled like whiskey and winking, and on that day it was filled with people who were filled with words. For five full hours, beginning in the afternoon and seeping into midnight, dozens of poets would cross the rickety stage on their way to the mic. The event, Neutral Turf, was a benefit for Guild Books, a venerable Chicago institution. It was also a balls-out attempt to pull together members of Chicago's fractured poetry community, which was in the midst of an unprecedented growth spurt. In its burgeoning midst were slammers and academes, formalists and freestylers, adolescents and orators, finger-pointers, ruthless competitors and unrepentant cravers of limelight. Everyone insisted that whatever *they* did was hotter, doper (that was a word then), more literate, relevant, contemporary, the next big thing. The organizers of Neutral Turf had devised an embarrassingly simple plan: get everyone mildly plastered and just giddy enough to realize that they were all doing the same damn thing.

I'm ashamed to admit it now, but I had come without words. My goal, as I remember it, was to drink heavily and laugh at poets. It was winter, which meant that Chi was a windy little ivory hell, and a five-hour respite—complete with blinking neon, warm drinks, and hilariously overwrought metaphors—was definitely in order. OK, I was young. I assumed poetry was relegated to a dusty bookshelf that I couldn't and didn't care to reach. I planned to guffaw heartily at odes to soulful flowers clawing their way up through cracks in the concrete.

I didn't know it yet, but Ms. Gwen was havin' none of that. She sat in the front row, head scarf triangled and tied, stockings rolled, specs riding her nose. I'm not sure how I knew she was who she was. (Later I learned that every Chicago colored girl is hardwired to recognize Gwendolyn Brooks on sight.) She paid rapt attention to just about every poet, smiling and nodding to rhythms, and making a small "O" sound when a line or phrase reached her in *that way*. During breaks, she nurtured the newbies, hugged when a hug was warranted, sipped at something icy and bland. Three of the five hours had passed, and she was still there, present in the soft but insistent way of the colored woman. Everywhere, gently, brashly.

When I approached her, I wasn't sure what I wanted. On a break between poets, I moved close and began, "Miss Brooks, I . . ." But a dreadlocked young woman—whose musical name, Inka Alasade, I remember to this day—had stepped to the mic and was about to begin her poem. Miss Brooks smiled and turned away from me to face the stage and listen. But she never let go of the hand I had extended in greeting: *I'm here. I'll be back. I am a vessel for what you need to say.*

So I held tight to what I did not yet know was a lifeline. I had come to drink and laugh out loud at a language I didn't think I needed to know, and now I held on as that language flowed from her fingers to mine.

I held on far beyond the eventual continuation of our conversation, during which I would begin to know poetry as necessary breath. I held tight past that day, that neon-splashed room, the procession of both fledgling and comfortably rooted writers. I clutched that knowing hand while my city finally acknowledged poetry as its heartbeat, as fractured elements forged an alliance and began to build one of the country's most formidable and adventurous creative communities. And in the center of that community, I burned like an ember, almost consumed by discovery.

I was from the West Side, the part of Chicago everyone tells you to stay away from. Gwendolyn lived on the South Side, where I was raised to believe the "bourgeoise" blacks resided. In Chicago terms, that can be two sides of a cultural and economic abyss. But I saw her often, usually at readings and events sponsored by Guild Books. In my hunger to be suddenly and completely immersed in all things literary and Chicago, I had volunteered to shelve books there on weekends. I met Eduardo Galeano. Guffawed heartily with Studs Terkel. And finally got to have my first real, unhurried conversation with Gwendolyn Brooks.

"I remember you," she said, just over my shoulder.

I turned around and hugged her, just like that. It was a rash, spontaneous clutch, a way to greet a childhood friend or a lost-ago aunt, not exactly the recommended hello for a casual acquaintance who just happened to be a former poet laureate and official Queen of the Colored Girl. For the moment, those three words legitimized me. She could conceivably have remembered me for my tendency to respond out loud at readings to poems that moved me, or for my habit of sitting up front and center, gazing gape-mouthed at my heroes. Maybe she was recalling Neutral Turf. But I wanted to think that she'd been in an audience somewhere and that I'd been onstage, that she'd heard something I said, and that she liked it. I wanted to believe that, so I didn't ask, just in case the answer was elsewhere.

We stood in a shadowed corner of the place while the busyness of a revolutionary bookstore went on around us. She pulled volumes down to show me, to tout the writer, to point to a favorite passage. We talked about Don L. Lee, Sterling Plumpp, Angela Jackson, Margaret Burroughs. I displayed an appalling lack of knowledge about what and who had come before me.

In my head swirled unrooted verses waiting for me to believe in them. My very first book, *Life According to Motown*, was still years away. It would be very much a first-generation-up-north book, a Chicago girl book, the first effort of a "stage poet" on the page, and it would come to exist primarily for two reasons:

1) Chicago stalwart Luis Rodriguez started Tia Chucha Books and asked me if I had a manuscript. Even though I didn't, I said yes.

2) What Gwendolyn Brooks said to me that day in Guild Books.

I had uttered something that countless other writers have uttered before, a silence-filler of sorts, a throat-clearing that I assumed Ms. Brooks, and anyone else who had ever picked up a pen, would instantly relate to and agree with. I was craving the comfort of common ground when I said, "I have a real problem finding time to write."

The corner of her mouth twitched, then spread into one of those indulgent smiles that knots you up a little inside. It's the smile a teacher gives you before handing back a test paper with a grade lower than either of you expected.

Without looking directly at me, Gwendolyn said, "Your problem should be finding time for anything else."

Silence, then. We continued to pluck certain books from certain shelves, examine glossy covers, read a little to ourselves. More people poured in, the program began, and she was quietly brilliant. When it was over and she was gone, I went home to my poems.

My poems, which suddenly *were* my home.

Patricia Smith

# The Golden Shovel
## by Terrance Hayes

*After Gwendolyn Brooks*

I. 1981

When I am so small Da's sock covers my arm, we
cruise at twilight until we find the place the real

men lean, bloodshot and translucent with cool.
His smile is a gold-plated incantation as we

drift by women on bar stools, with nothing left
in them but approachlessness. This is a school

I do not know yet. But the cue sticks mean we
are rubbed by light, smooth as wood, the lurk

of smoke thinned to song. We won't be out late.
Standing in the middle of the street last night we

watched the moonlit lawns and a neighbor strike
his son in the face. A shadow knocked straight

Da promised to leave me everything: the shovel we
used to bury the dog, the words he loved to sing

his rusted pistol, his squeaky Bible, his sin.
The boy's sneakers were light on the road. We

watched him run to us looking wounded and thin.
He'd been caught lying or drinking his father's gin.

He'd been defending his ma, trying to be a man. We
stood in the road, and my father talked about jazz,

how sometimes a tune is born of outrage. By June
the boy would be locked upstate. That night we

got down on our knees in my room. If I should die
before I wake. Da said to me, it will be too soon.


## II. 1991

Into the tented city we go, we-
akened by the fire's ethereal

afterglow. Born lost and cool-
er than heartache. What we

know is what we know. The left
hand severed and school-

ed by cleverness. A plate of we-
ekdays cooking. The hour lurk-

ing in the afterglow. A late-
night chant. Into the city we

go. Close your eyes and strike
a blow. Light can be straight-

ened by its shadow. What we
break is what we hold. A sing-

ular blue note. An outcry sin-
ged exiting the throat. We

push until we thin, thin-
king we won't creep back again.

While God licks his kin, we
sing until our blood is jazz,

we swing from June to June.
We sweat to keep from we-

eping. Groomed on a die-
t of hunger, we end too soon.

# Selected Poems by Gwendolyn Brooks

## A Sunset of the City

*Kathleen Eileen*

Already I am no longer looked at with lechery or love.
My daughters and sons have put me away with marbles and dolls,
Are gone from the house.
My husband and lovers are pleasant or somewhat polite
And night is night.

It is a real chill out,
The genuine thing.
I am not deceived, I do not think it is still summer
Because sun stays and birds continue to sing.

It is summer-gone that I see, it is summer-gone.
The sweet flowers indrying and dying down,
The grasses forgetting their blaze and consenting to brown.

It is a real chill out. The fall crisp comes.
I am aware there is winter to heed.
There is no warm house
That is fitted with my need.
I am cold in this cold house this house
Whose washed echoes are tremulous down lost halls.
I am a woman, and dusty, standing among new affairs.
I am a woman who hurries through her prayers.

Tin intimations of a quiet core to be my
Desert and my dear relief
Come: there shall be such islanding from grief,
And small communion with the master shore.
Twang they. And I incline this ear to tin,
Consult a dual dilemma. Whether to dry
In humming pallor or to leap and die.

Somebody muffed it? Somebody wanted to joke.

xlviii    Selected Poems by Gwendolyn Brooks

## kitchenette building

We are things of dry hours and the involuntary plan,
Grayed in, and gray. "Dream" makes a giddy sound, not strong
Like "rent," "feeding a wife," "satisfying a man."

But could a dream send up through onion fumes
Its white and violet, fight with fried potatoes
And yesterday's garbage ripening in the hall,
Flutter, or sing an aria down these rooms

Even if we were willing to let it in,
Had time to warm it, keep it very clean,
Anticipate a message, let it begin?

We wonder. But not well! not for a minute!
Since Number Five is out of the bathroom now,
We think of lukewarm water, hope to get in it.

## Boy Breaking Glass

*To Marc Crawford*
*from whom the commission*

Whose broken window is a cry of art
(success, that winks aware
as elegance, as a treasonable faith)
is raw: is sonic: is old-eyed première.
Our beautiful flaw and terrible ornament.
Our barbarous and metal little man.

"I shall create! If not a note, a hole.
If not an overture, a desecration."

Full of pepper and light
and salt and night and cargoes.

"Don't go down the plank
if you see there's no extension.
Each to his grief, each to
his loneliness and fidgety revenge.
Nobody knew where I was and now I am no longer there."

The only sanity is a cup of tea.
The music is in minors.

Each one other
is having different weather.

"It was you, it was you who threw away my name!
And this is everything I have for me."

Who has not Congress, lobster, love, luau,
the Regency Room, the Statue of Liberty,
runs. A sloppy amalgamation.
A mistake.
A cliff.
A hymn, a snare, and an exceeding sun.

**a song in the front yard**

I've stayed in the front yard all my life.
I want a peek at the back
Where it's rough and untended and hungry weed grows.
A girl gets sick of a rose.

I want to go in the back yard now
And maybe down the alley,
To where the charity children play.
I want a good time today.

They do some wonderful things.
They have some wonderful fun.
My mother sneers, but I say it's fine
How they don't have to go in at quarter to nine.
My mother, she tells me that Johnnie Mae
Will grow up to be a bad woman.
That George'll be taken to Jail soon or late
(On account of last winter he sold our back gate).

But I say it's fine. Honest, I do.
And I'd like to be a bad woman, too,
And wear the brave stockings of night-black lace
And strut down the streets with paint on my face.

## The Bean Eaters

They eat beans mostly, this old yellow pair.
Dinner is a casual affair.
Plain chipware on a plain and creaking wood,
Tin flatware.

Two who are Mostly Good.
Two who have lived their day,
But keep on putting on their clothes
And putting things away.

And remembering . . .
Remembering, with twinklings and twinges,
As they lean over the beans in their rented back room that is full of beads and
    receipts and dolls and cloths, tobacco crumbs, vases and fringes.

Poems reprinted from *Selected Poems,* published by Harper & Row. Copyright © 1963 by
Gwendolyn Brooks. Reprinted with the permission of the Estate of Gwendolyn Brooks.

The Golden Shovel Anthology

# The Anniad

## ARACELIS GIRMAY

Aracelis Girmay is an educator and writer. She is the author of *Changing, Changing; Teeth; Kingdom Animalia*, and *The Black Maria*. She teaches at Hampshire College.

### After

We remember to be what the sumac made us: lit with red life,
the holler of survivor's blood—but what was
our name when we were green? When History was little?

Species by species, we inch the tightrope, thinly-together. As
siblings. Every now & then stopping for our eyes to follow, into dark space, a
brother who wouldn't last. Though we throw our songs down after, the relatives—
    now little bones, & sand.

―――――――

## HAILEY LEITHAUSER

Hailey Leithauser is the author of *Swoop* (Graywolf Press, 2013). Her work appears widely in journals and anthologies including *Agni, Field, Gettysburg Review, Poetry,* and *Yale Review* and has been featured in three editions of *Best American Poetry.*

### What There Is to Spend

What there is to spend is not yet spent
and moon lifts golden for girl and wench,
golden with dance, honeyed with whiskey
and scented hand and coin and glance and . . .
until morning swing its devil tail
and whiskey and dance and moon-gelt end.

# Appendix to the Anniad

## PAUL MARTINEZ-POMPA

Paul Martinez-Pompa is the author of *My Kill Adore Him*, which won the Andres Montoya Poetry Prize. He is also a recipient of an Illinois Arts Council award. He earned degrees from the University of Chicago and Indiana University. Currently, he edits for *Packingtown Review* and teaches at Triton College.

### Next Time Honey

Like moonlight, I'll slip out before
you stagger home with your

hands & fists, your song of horror
no throat nor eye-socket can

mute. I'll be back with a pistol. Be
ready, baby. Be ready for somethin' sweet.

———

## RACHEL RICHARDSON

Rachel Richardson is the author of *Copperhead* (2011) and *Hundred-Year Wave* (2016), both in the Carnegie Mellon Poetry Series. A recent National Endowment for the Arts and Stegner Fellow, she writes prose for the Poetry Foundation and Kenyon Review Online, and her poetry appears in *Slate, New England Review*, and elsewhere.

### A Halo for Her Invisible Hair

There's nothing left to do about the bees
that cloak the table and sofa, dazed in
the work of bowing, of occupying the
dusky space, its vessels. As the stomach
aches for its milk. Swarm. Not sweat

of labor, nor voices calling—a hum across
a calm tableau. *You, come here to me*, the
weary woman used to say. Creased brow.
Worn hands. Bees mass in her armchair. *Come now.*

# The Artists' and Models' Ball

## ANNE SHAW

Alix Anne Shaw is the author of two poetry collections: *Dido in Winter* (Persea, 2014) and *Undertow* (Persea, 2007), winner of the Lexi Rudnitsky Poetry Prize. Her poems and reviews have appeared in journals including *Harvard Review, Black Warrior Review, Denver Quarterly, Los Angeles Review,* and *New American Writing.* Her work is online at anneshaw.org.

### Weather Report

The city ices in at one degree. One must accept such wonders
till they cease. What ruckuses of weather. What to-do.
Friend, here's what I know of the mayfly, pressing its thorax hard against the
    screen. It is not
so much location as the problem of bodies in space. How we confuse
the chair for armature, mistake the frosted window for the sea. We
stay in separate cities and winter salts its skin. These days, whatever call
I hear is what I answer to. The trees, though I do not know them.
The men who trouble the alley. The trucks. It has come to that.

# An Aspect of Love, Alive in the Ice and Fire

## PATTIANN ROGERS

Pattiann Rogers has published fourteen books, most recently *Holy Heathen Rhapsody* (Penguin, 2013). She is the recipient of two National Endowment for the Arts Grants, a Guggenheim Fellowship, and a Lannan Literary Award in Poetry. Her poems have received five Pushcart Prizes, two appearances in *Best American Poetry*, and five appearances in *Best Spiritual Writing*.

### First Summer Song

I keep the window curtains open all day because
the violet morning glory vines are climbing up the
panes now; and, hidden in the blossoming spirea, a world

waking in the grass-woven nest of the song sparrow is
noisy with burgeoning and birth; and because the sun is at
its most celestial summer glory; and because the

baby and you, my world, love watching at the window.

---

## RENÉE WATSON

Renée Watson is a poet and author of children's books. Her books include *This Side of Home* and *Harlem's Little Blackbird: The Story of Florence Mills*. Her work has received several honors including an National Association for the Advancement of Colored People Image Award nomination. She has given readings and lectures at many renowned places, including the United Nations and the Library of Congress.

### An Aspect of Love

My mother is a gospel hymn, is the altar's moan. We
baptize each other in a mosaic of testimony. Her laugh

survived girlhood, Jim Crow, divorce, welfare, cancer. We
sit on the porch under shawl of summer sunset. I touch
her past, count the deaths and births of dreams. Feel each
and every scar. I reveal mine and one story heals the other.

# Ballad of Pearl May Lee

## SUSAN WHEELER

Susan Wheeler is the author of six books of poetry, most recently *Meme* (University of Iowa), and a novel, *Record Palace* (Graywolf Press). The recipient of a Guggenheim Fellowship and the Witter Bynner Prize for Poetry from the American Academy of Arts and Letters, she teaches at Princeton University.

### Stay, Dear

Take the noose from the pocket of your robe—I
won't keep you longer than it will take to cut
the muck from your rheumy
eyes. I'm sick for the loosening spit of your lungs,
the animal's skull your hulk has become, with
its sorry-ass terrace above the stream Styx my
land here abuts. Stay this side. Know laughter.

# The Ballad of Rudolph Reed

## ANDREW MOTION

Andrew Motion is a Homewood Professor in the Arts at Johns Hopkins
University. He was the poet laureate of the United Kingdom from 1999 to 2009.

## Conjunction

I rejected every conjunction except 'and'
at precisely the same time you pressed
into my life. Likewise I chose to use 'the'
not 'a' or 'an', when I felt your slim hand
taking a hold of my hand to give proof of
your thinking I was no longer 'him' or 'his'
but 'mine'. 'Mine' as in 'husband and wife'.

# The Bean Eaters

## BONNIE JO CAMPBELL

Bonnie Campbell wrote *Mothers, Tell Your Daughters* and *Once upon a River*. She was a National Book Award finalist for her collection, *American Salvage*, as well as a Guggenheim fellow. Her poetry chapbook *Love Letters to Sons of Bitches* won the Center for Book Arts award. She lives in Kalamazoo.

### Resurrection

Garbage men rumble and rattle the sunrise service as they
toss into their truck the moveable feast we did not eat.

In hats and gloves they haul away daffodils and jelly beans,
parade away carcasses of ham and roast lamb. Mostly

we don't save our scraps or boil our bones, but we tried this
Easter to make a religion of shaking hands. We fed the old

ladies cake until they rose from the dead to shine yellow
light on little girls' shoes, making perfect each cheap pair.

---

## CAITLIN DOYLE

Caitlin Doyle's poetry has appeared in several journals, magazines, and anthologies, including *The Atlantic, Threepenny Review, Boston Review*, and *Best New Poets*. She has received a Bread Loaf Writers' Conference scholarship, a MacDowell fellowship, the Amy Award through *Poets and Writers*, a James Merrill House fellowship, and others.

### The Parrot Man

Newlyweds can't resist him, just a buck or two
for one snapshot. Even middle-aged couples who

hardly keep island vacation albums anymore are
charmed by his rum-barrel belly, though mostly
it's his bird their cameras want—a scene as good
as any postcard: perched on his arm with two-
toned tail feathers flashing for travelers who
have finally arrived. He knows they couldn't have
dreamt a brighter bird (or dream how it lived
in a poacher's basement, before it was his) for their
dollar. Dressed in the same Aloha shirt every day,
he could almost be mistaken for another tourist but
for the kids surrounding him—"How do you keep
it from getting away? "Does it talk?" "Will it sit on
my arm?" He tells it to speak, but there's no putting
words in its mouth. If only he could teach it to perch on
other people—twice the tips! All it does is shriek at their
outstretched hands, shake its beak, stain their clothes
with droppings if they get too close. Yet they still stand
around as if it might let itself be touched—as if putting
money in the cup won't make it think that something's
come to kill it—clipped wings fluttering to fly away.

———————

## SANDRA M. GILBERT

Sandra M. Gilbert has published eight collections of poetry—most recently
*Aftermath* (2011)—and among prose books *Wrongful Death, Death's Door,
Rereading Women*, and, in 2014, *The Culinary Imagination: From Myth to
Modernity*. With longtime collaborator Susan Gubar, she received the 2012
Award for Lifetime Achievement from the National Book Critics Circle.

### The Fava Bean-Eaters

We're dining at Frangipane—and who are they
peering through plate glass to watch us drink and eat?

We nibble gravlax, pureed fava beans,
The colors here are cream & crimson, mostly.

Here's Breton lobster salad, shall we share this?
The sommelier pours wine; outside, the old

too shabby couple gazes at my yellow
curls.
     Why do they peep–that filthy pair?

_____

## NIKKI GIOVANNI

Poet Nikki Giovanni was born in Knoxville, Tennessee, on June 7, 1943. Although she grew up in Cincinnati, Ohio, she and her sister returned to Knoxville each summer to visit their grandparents. Nikki graduated with honors in history from her grandfather's alma mater, Fisk University. Since 1987, she has been on the faculty at Virginia Tech, where she is a university distinguished professor.

### At the Evening of Life

I wonder if they
See the evening of life as a treat to eat
Or as a staple like beans
With corn bread mostly
A good warming meal this
Daily day old
Bread pudding love capped sunshine yellow
By an honest upstanding pair

_____

## DIANE GLANCY

Diane Glancy is professor emerita at Macalester College. Her 2014–15 books, *Fort Marion Prisoners and the Trauma of Native Education*, nonfiction, University of Nebraska Press; *Report to the Department of the Interior*, poetry, University of New Mexico Press; and *Uprising of Goats, One of Us*, and *Ironic Witness*, novels, Wipf and Stock. www.dianeglancy.org.

## Evening

In the evening they
sit at the table and eat
potatoes and beans
preferring mostly
the familiar quiet of this
knife, this fork, this old
burning of late yellow
light candled on the pair.

---

## JACK POWERS

Jack Powers's poems have appeared in *Southern Review, Southern Poetry Review, Rattle, Poet Lore, Cortland Review,* and elsewhere. He teaches at Joel Barlow High School in Redding, Connecticut. More at: www.jackpowers13.com/poetry.

## Roadside Diner: Fairfield, Maine

Like a depression era painting by a lesser Rockwell, a pale, veined couple pause
    mid-meal. They
hunch over the chipped Formica table. Behind them, words painted on the
    window say, "EAT,"
backwards in blue. They squint, spoons in mid-air, steam rising off the brown
    beans
as if she's said something important about the grandchildren or the crops, and he
    nods—mostly
to stall for time, mostly to avoid a scene in public, mostly to eat the beans while
    they're hot. This
moment caught over my wife's shoulder lingers as she stirs her coffee and talks
    again about how old
our own children have become, how our job has changed to listening. We move
    into the yellow
of mid-day, drive down the Maine coast and as the fog rolls in, hurtle through the
    souped-up air.

## CHRISTIAN ROBINSON

Christian Robinson (Rich Robbins), is a hip-hop recording artist out of Chicago. In 2012 Rich was accepted into First Wave, a full-tuition hip-hop scholarship to the University of Wisconsin. His art narrates a young Brown man with homes in urban and suburban communities, thus Rich's art is a means of bridging those worlds.

### Next to the Flatware

Now, my grandmother forgets to mention "they"
when she speaks of my parents. As if now, you eat
and consume them separately. A Mexican bean.
And a Black bean. From same family but mostly
on different ends of the garden. It's strange how this

walking from one end to the other has become natural.
The flowers between them have grown old.
Lost all their yellow.
How much distance does it take to stop qualifying as a pair?

Last night we had beans for dinner.
They were refried. We ate twice. A pair. Is
natural. Grandmother forgets. Maybe because she's old. Wilting. A
memory can be as casual
as a bean. Having an affair
with the ground. Forgotten by the one that picked it. It's too plain.

It doesn't stand out like last night's chipware.
It doesn't stand out like two beans on
a garden. They began at A.
Good starting point. And now sit at opposite ends of the plain.
Grandmother says they are dying out and
the dinner table keeps growing out. Creaking.
With every movement of its wood.

Maybe they would have lasted if they had been found in tin.
Store bought instead of homemade. Next to the flatware.

## PHILIP SCHULTZ

Philip Schultz's most recent book is a novel in verse, *The Wherewithal* (W. W. Norton, 2014). His collection, *Failure*, won the 2008 Pulitzer Prize in poetry. He founded and directs the Writers Studio, a private school for fiction and poetry with branches in New York, Tucson, San Francisco, Amsterdam, and online.

### New Year's Eve in Times Square

Time was when everything wasn't now, remembering
the waltzing dead, stubborn with panache, with
something to prove, promises un-kept, twinklings
of fate: eight seven . . . five . . . father holding me high and
mother's sad expectant eyes, horns jubilant, in twinges.

# Beverly Hills, Chicago

## DIDI JACKSON

Didi Jackson's poems have appeared or are forthcoming in *Ploughshares, Green Mountains Review*, the *Common, Solstice, Passages North*, and *Sierra Nevada Review*. Her chapbook, *Slag and Fortune*, was published by Floating Wolf Quarterly in 2013. She divides her time between Florida and Vermont, teaching at the University of Central Florida and at the University of Vermont.

### Golden Shovel Buddha

A warrior I am not, even when
I try my hardest. I am a disciple of we,
a follower of union, and I speak
clearly of the rickshaw of love to
anyone who will listen. Each
of us must come to the edge of the other
either in this life or the next. Ours
is a marriage sifted from mistakes and old voices
ticked like a wristwatch: a reminder we are
on a well-worn path, king-sized and cherry like a
carved Buddha reclining in a gift shop window whose little
hands are like all hands, full of patience and a little gruff.

## MAJOR JACKSON

Major Jackson is the author of *Roll Deep* (Norton, 2015). He is a recipient of a Guggenheim Fellowship, a Pushcart Prize, a Whiting Writers' Award. Jackson is the Richard A. Dennis Green and Gold Professor at the University of Vermont.

### Stand Your Ground

America, how often I have applauded your flag-poles. We,
as citizens, struggle to find common ground, yet do

much to damage the planks of your Ark. Not
a soft tune we make, glissando of the harmonized. We have a want
problem: more of ourselves problem, Us versus Them
in the great race to prosperity. In his Introduction to
Metaphysics, Heidegger asks "Why are there beings at all?" We have
as guides: Klansmen and eugenicists, where The Other is less.
It is, I admit, the slapping of your ropes tolling a perfect union. But,
is the measure of your worth a silent clang elsewhere? How is it
a ripple runs through me when the wind rises? A cloth is
nation, hauled down or half-mast, like a deferred dream only
earthly because we strive on a path hidden by dead leaves, a natural
entity whose death makes valid its rebirth,—that
an angry man can shoot a teenager is par, as we say. We,
Iota, Sigma, Tau, Deltas, new tribesmen in new codes, should
in earnest put away our swords and talk-shows. Think:
our watermelons have so many seeds, and we,
galaxy in us, dissolve like lumps of wax. The mysteries we have,
an unmitigated burning of sound and fury, not
organism of one, but organs. America, I've had enough.

---

## ANGELA NARCISO TORRES

Angela Narciso Torres's book *Blood Orange* won the Willow Books Literature Award. Recent work appears in *Colorado Review, Drunken Boat*, and *Cimarron Review*. Angela has received fellowships from Bread Loaf Writers' Conference, Illinois Arts Council, and Ragdale. A *RHINO Poetry* editor and Warren Wilson MFA graduate, she lives in Chicago.

### September, Chicago

There's a coolness—almost metallic—in the air, even
    though the almanac says eleven days till fall. But the
birch trees are impossibly green and the only leaves

turning are these blue-lined pages. Windblown, they fall
    open to where I erased your name. I go down
to the basement, unpack your letters, still bound in

summer's heat. Was your script always lovelier
    under a bare bulb? Light bleeds patterns
through ink & paper, spiral glyphs spelling, *Wait. Still here.*

# The Birth in a Narrow Room

## JENNY BOULLY

Jenny Boully is the author of *Not Merely Because of the Unknown That Was Stalking Toward Them*, *The Book of Beginnings and Endings: Essays*, *The Body: An Essay*, and other works.

### Child Tipping Forever

*She frets and twists, resists having her hair in twines,*
*will not sit still to endure the hair brushing, and*
*I can only reproach her tantrums weakly,*
*succumb to alternatives of grooming.* Her baby doll winks
and poops and pees and sleeps upon
its own little baby doll bed. I cannot get my
little girl to empty her milk-glass
to eat the carrots or potatoes or even any fruit
and there still sits the cold and brimming bowl
of oats and raisins. I cannot remember the last time I had time to iron
slacks and shirts. I have too long left the soaking pot
in the sink overnight. I have neglected to count the
pennies accumulating. She grows bashful
when I peek at her in ballet class. My wedding china
is not, never was china and breaks daily. My child
still wants to be held like a baby, her head a flower tipping
towards her bedtime pillow, a reminder that forever
is forever gone from me. The mint is turning yellow
and I have lost the one good apron
that my mother gave to me and
no matter what the cups in this house keep spilling.
She's in her tutu and twirling and her pretty
sunshine arms refuse the dear cherries.

# The Blackstone Rangers

## JUDY BLUNDELL

Judy Blundell is a writer for young adults. Her novel, *What I Saw and How I Lied*, won the National Book Award for Young People's Literature in 2008.

What is betrayal but a construct?
A thing she built of sludge and salt, strangely
solid, as real as the rabbit in the hat, a
spiel, a sleight, the flourish *ta-da* monstrous
to all but her. She sets her teeth to nacre not to test the pearl
but enjoy the taste of mineral, or
scrape it down to nub, swallow, and think it grace.

---

## CHELSEA DIXON

Chelsea Dixon wrote this poem when she was a freshman at Oak Park and River Forest High School. She was a three-time member of the Louder than a Bomb slam team. She is now a freshman at Long Island University.

### The Ache

You can take away the ache, but it takes time for the sores.
Cocoa butter can't pretty these. Growing up in
bruises Jose leaves from baseball bats reminds me the
reason I shoved him down the stairs. Why was this? In the city
I'm from, it wasn't ok to have Mexican friends. I'm told that
since slavery is over, so is racism. This is my normal. We do
these things. My teacher, Ms. Shannon does not
know, black is the color shedding blood on walls that don't want
to speak. Walls protect secrets running through them. It takes time to
fade away the ache. It takes time to heal.

## RANDALL HORTON

Randall Horton is the recipient of the Gwendolyn Brooks Poetry Award and a National Endowment of the Arts Fellowship in Literature. Triquarterly/ Northwestern published his latest poetry collection *Pitch Dark Anarchy. Hook: A Memoir* is forthcoming from Augury Books. Randall is associate professor of English at the University of New Haven.

## A Love Jones in a Booming Economy

at precisely eleven thirty
a torrential downpour at
play, line to the
block, around the corner,
all faces black
prepare to purchase heroin, raw
uncut, *jones* at the ready—

## QURAYSH ALI LANSANA

Quraysh Ali Lansana teaches at the School of the Art Institute of Chicago and is the author of eighteen books—most recently, *The BreakBeat Poets: New American Poetry in the Age of Hip Hop.* His forthcoming titles include *The Whiskey of Our Discontent: Gwendolyn Brooks as Conscience and Change Agent* and *Revise the Psalm: Writing Inspired by the Work of Gwendolyn Brooks.*

## 1972 ford ltd

a harvest gold & avocado green leisure suit with fm radio, it was their,
well, daddy's, mansion, his james brown conk cool, his funky country
on radials, power windows and doors a working class music. here is
our block-long plush, envy of uncles and teenage dolemite dreams. a
ms. cleopatra jones ride, showing yankees, john denver, the hippie nation
and everyone except texas the middle finger. kept the 25 gallon tank on
full. we drove to kentucky for my sister's wedding on hot backroads, no
cracker corn farmer's rifle loud enough to make daddy use a map.

## MIKE PUICAN

Mike Puican has had poems in *Poetry, Michigan Quarterly Review,* and *New England Review,* among others. His poetry reviews have appeared in *Kenyon Review* and *TriQuarterly.* Mike was member of the 1996 Chicago Slam Team and for ten years has been board president of the Guild Literary Complex in Chicago.

## FUNERAL Sign

Dream-brimmed and impatient, and there-
fore left face-up in Jeremiah Black's back alley. They

accepted his mother's old coins for the burial. T-shirts are
are printed and distributed to the thirty

or forty thousand who scrape by only to lose a son at
2 a.m. on his way to the Green Line. A six-year-old places the

FUNERAL sign in each windshield's lower right-hand corner.
Last week, released from the police station, he wiped the black

ink from his fingerprints and stepped out into the raw
winter night—landing in someone's kitchen, ready

for anything that would change the luck in the room. Open sores
pock the neighborhood most every afternoon in

the form of processions crawling through streets that still hold the
certain rumple of his jacket, the tap of his hand to music, his city-

wide, street-wise smile, still hold his mother's sweet talk that
never left him, never left him for dead, still hold the men who do

not have options but have the need to take action, who do not
believe things will change, who do not want

forgiveness. Their lives, dream-brimmed and short, add to
the processions of voices calling out to those who are left—heal!

## KELLY REUTER

Kelly Reuter is from Oak Park Illinois. She is a student at Benedictine University working on her BA in English literature. She was a semifinalist for the Gwendolyn Brooks Open Mic Award in 2014. She has taught poetry workshops and performed her original work all over Chicago.

### After the Eulogy

She thinks my brother is still lying there.
His pants tucked over his shoes. They
kiss the ground like prayer knees and are
the closest he's ever been to God. Thirty-
five this year but, he's still just dragging. At
sunrise, my mom takes walks down the
block. I know she's still looking. At the corner
she counts his age in bricks of gum: black
and stuck. I count them too. Instead: ageless, raw,
infinity. Not ready for caskets. Not ready
to become one of our sores.
I squint my eyes and try to imagine being in
a place that hasn't taken the
corpse of the city
and hung it by each of its limbs. That
place is where he is now. I know this, but I do
not know how come my mom does not.
She has been searching for his stillness. I want
her to lull him from the pavement; to
make doves from concrete. To heal.

## NATALIE RICHARDSON

Natalie Richardson is a fourth-year student at the University of Chicago, studying cinema and media studies and comparative race and ethnic studies. An alumna of the National Student Poets Program and a recipient of the Seidel Scholar's Grant, Natalie hopes to combine her love of writing with her interest in film by pursuing a career in screenwriting and directing.

## Cure and Curry

My father is a nod, a jilt. Bop.
Insists that 90s music is the jams they
will drop when I have children. Cancel
the station with rap-crap, the cure
for stiff-skin is the blunk of funk and
lilt of lips that pickles like sound-curry.

----------

## DEBRIS STEVENSON

Finding poetry enabled Debris to decipher her dyslexia. Since, she's been followed
by Channel4, published by the likes of Magma and Louis Vuitton, and had her
debut pamphlet, *Pigeon Party*, released by Flipped Eye. Founder/artistic director
of the Mouth Poets, Debris is developing a Grime/Poetry exchange project
following a series of commissions from BBC 1xtra.

## i. Cecil Park—High as the Swings

They were teaching me how to roll up. There,
on the swings, everyone was learning. They
were grey Pitbulls going for an un-bagged shit. "Are
we drinking enough?" One asks, as thirty
sheets of Rizla angel from my fingers. The wind at
1am, weed rolled loose as a Tesco bag, the
polystyrene cup cracked under our teeth. In the corner

sharing headphones, listening to Dizzee's black
vibrations, backs of our heads touching. Raw
rum laughing. As our throats throb ready
smoke. Sitting on the swings, the 8 year old sores
scabbed and pickable, worth the scars set in
memories that fit on fingers like Hoola-Hoops. The
lighters set fire to bins for warmth and jokes. The city—
a shitty sun. We've needed a new one for a while—that
doesn't soak into the tarmac like chewing gum. Do

we feel cold? Our skin does but our mind's do not . . .
like scotch bonnets. I ask, "Is this what we want?"
They walk their swings to tip toe. Jump-ready. Aiming to
the suspicious sun. We'd do anything. Anything, to heal.

## ii. Dutch Pot Dancing

In the back of a Dutch Pot shop, 200 sweating bodies hardly
smell of anything. It's a happy stink. We're Belafonte
banana boats inventing Calypso with motions. Kings
of testosterone. We pack in until even the air is Black.
Hair new and waxed. We are happy being 16, as Jesus
might have been. Singing "follow the leader." Leaders, Stokely,
presidents of panther mentality, beautiful as violent Malcolm
when he was real-life-living, before the power of X.

Pelvises kissing. I haven't drunk or smoked a thing or
had time to decide if I want to. Hips learning flow like rap.
Little boys learn to hold bigger girls. Heads bungled
into pink lace front wigs, passing out plastic-cup-punch trophies,
smells of bass, tastes of steamed up windows. Synchronized. Their
feet drawing patterns like 8 year old fingers from car seats. A country
made of multi-coloured beats. Fenugreek and clove over meat is
sometimes enough for peace and a party. Enough for me to be a
dancehall queen. Enough for all of us to taste at home in a nation
where statistics can only expose a cocktail-stick. I lead the chants on
"Trinidad . . . follow the leader . . . raise ya' hand . . . love and unity." No
one can shout louder. But everyone can add a new move to our map.

# Boy Breaking Glass

## MEENA ALEXANDER

Meena Alexander's seven books of poetry include the PEN Award–winning
book of poems *Illiterate Heart* and *Birthplace with Buried Stones,* (published by
TriQuarterly Books/ Northwestern University Press). She is the editor of *Indian
Love Poems*. She is distinguished professor of English, Graduate Center/ Hunter
College, City University of New York. meenaalexander.com.

### Imagine This

In the last year of my life I'll make a
house of words and with it a hymn
of barbed wire, bandits in velvet masks, a
fiction of ancient walls and painted ponds (surely a snare
for love). Also calligraphy of copper wire,
couplets in so many half-known tongues: I'll reach for an
atlas of broken syntax far exceeding
what one might long for in a wintry sun.

## CATHERINE BROGAN

Cat Brogan is a spoken word educator with an MA from Goldsmiths. Originally
from Northern Ireland, Cat won the BBC Edinburgh Fringe Poetry Slam
and has appeared at festivals in the United Kingdom and internationally. Her
students' performances have included the House of Parliament and have won
awards with Adobe and the United Nations.

### Boys Breaking Glass

The boys' snowballs shattered the window. I
told dad. My cousin mooned them. We shall
make the parents pay, for what they create!
The quiet one now runs the family gallery. If

I see the younger brother, though I hope not
to, will he produce a recompense for pinning a
teenage me, to my parents' bed? An apology note,
a reparation? I didn't tell dad that time, that a
boy cracked our space, crafted a silent hole.

----

## HANNAH GAMBLE

Hannah Gamble is the author of *Your Invitation to a Modest Breakfast* (Fence Books, 2012). She lives in Chicago.

Asked why I always have to be so negative I
say "Well, mother, why don't you look at my genitals? Then you shall
see I've been asked to make something from nothing—given a hole from which to
    create!"
And *that* will only happen if I choose to make a child or venereal disease—if,
that is, there's a gentleman willing to aid me. Fortunately it's not
at all unusual for a convex to help a concave. Just like a
bottle of wine is happy to help the glass overflow (or, on a more anatomical note,
take more dick than you ever thought possible all thanks to insistence). You know, a
wineglass sometimes consoles itself, thinking how its slender stem makes it more
    than just a hole.

----

## M. AYODELE HEATH

Atlanta native M. Ayodele Heath is author of *Otherness* (Brick Road Poetry Press) and editor of the anthology of collaborative poems, *Electronic Corpse: Poems from a Digital Salon* (Svaha Paradox). Ayo holds an MFA in poetry from New England College and is a former McEver Visiting Chair in Writing at Georgia Tech.

## Ornithology

*For Charlie Parker*

Hole-in-the-wall is how the uninitiated might describe the Kansas City club where I,
a one-winged flight of drunken tap dancer, become Bird. Ornithology shall
note the lightning-quick riffs I saxophone through the ivory teeth of time to create

a sound so jazzed it might leave even Roach writhing in the dust. What is bebop, if
not staggering chords of a sky-high God marionetting a poppy's bloom? Forgive
    me not
if my embouchure's notes frantically flap to keep from crashing in a
create-art-from-crash-&-burn world. Can't you hear me reaching up? No note
shall go unturned as I fall, 1,000 screams per second, obliterating the key of A.
I ain't your dance music; I'm a hummingbird's wings breaking: Needle, vein, hole.

_____

## PAM HOUSTON

Pam Houston is the author of five books of fiction and nonfiction including
*Cowboys Are My Weakness* and *Contents May Have Shifted*, all published by
W. W. Norton. She teaches at the Institute of American Indian Arts, University
of California Davis and directs the literary nonprofit, Writing by Writers.

### Behind in the Count

A few miles from Oracle Arizona, in the
dead of winter (weeks before Spring training) a man who was only
five feet tall saved my sanity.
What's your name, he said, as he set h(is)
own shirt on fire and then began to keen like a
bird, or like a man who has lost his last cup
of money.            Later, during mettā meditation, I thought only of
(you) (you). Only blocks from the ballpark, high tea
in Lo-hi, snow falling around the
mast that holds no sail.            At middle age, this sweet strange Music
of acceptance. A World Series of bad decisions behind us, it is
work & road trips, powder days & playlists we put our trust in—
(prudent) like two former MVP's sent down to pitch out our careers in the minors

_____

## TROY JOLLIMORE

Troy Jollimore is the author of three collections of poetry: *Tom Thomson in
Purgatory* (2006), *At Lake Scugog* (2011), and *Syllabus of Errors*. (2015). His
awards include the National Book Critics Circle Award and fellowships from the
Bread Loaf Writers' Conference and the Guggenheim Foundation.

### Sleeping under Stars

So he slept in the courtyard, wondering whose
tears she'd been crying in the kitchen, what broken
melody the misaligned birds at the window
had been disharmoniously bleating. The May sky is
etched with luminous names, he noticed; a
devil might offer to weld a man's cry
to the lovelorn, soulsick, heartbroken song of
the stars. But the stars' songs lie. Pain is not art.

---

### PHILIP LEVINE

Philip Levine won several awards, including the National Book Award, the National Books Critics Circle award, the Pulitzer Prize, Ruth Lilly Prize in Poetry, and the Wallace Stevens Award. In 2011 he was appointed poet laureate of the United States. Levine retired from teaching at the California State University, Fresno in 1992. He split his time between Fresno and Brooklyn in his later years, before his death in early 2015.

### The Second Going

Again the
day begins, only
no one wants its sanity
or its blinding clarity. Daylight is
not what we came all this way for. A
pinch of salt, a drop of schnapps in our cup
of tears, the ticket to the life to come, a short life of
long nights & absent dawns & a little mercy in the tea.

---

### ERIKA MEITNER

Erika Meitner is the author of four books of poems, including *Copia* (BOA Editions, 2014), and *Ideal Cities* (Harper Perennial, 2010), which was a 2009 National Poetry Series winner. She is currently an associate professor of English at Virginia Tech, where she directs the MFA program in creative writing.

## Meadowlands

The lines are long and it's Friday and
they say you must wait or come back and salt
goes into the pot, dissolves same as sugar and

everywhere is equally dark at night
once the blue hour passes and

someone cradles us like water, like cargoes
of pylons and smokestacks which don't
emit light but send signals of vapor that go

out to sea like breath in winter. You are down
the shore where everything is all right. The

radio sings static. Two boys fish on a plank
jutting out from the sand. You don't ask if
they've caught anything today since you

see their empty bucket. You see
their too-short pants. Some days there's

no telling what will bite: weakfish, bluefish, no
tired shoes or message bottles offering an extension
of kindness, a cry, a reaching out from each

car that journeys the turnpike with lit eyes to
show a boy the measure of his shadow, his

airplane roar—his shame or grief
a place to pass through, a place each
of us buries or forgets on the way to

somewhere else: this fuselage, this
stump, this swamp, this loneliness.

## MICHAEL MEYERHOFER

Michael Meyerhofer's most recent book of poetry is *What to Do if You're Buried Alive*. He is also the author of a fantasy trilogy and serves as the poetry editor of *Atticus Review*. For more information and at least one embarrassing childhood photo, please visit troublewithhammers.com.

### Opening Ceremonies, 2012

How they wave their cell phones at stadiums full
of flash bulbs and the hand-drawn banners of
those who could afford the airfare, pepper
of so many bodyguards in suits and
earpieces, London's first applause of light
overshadowing a bored queen while we drunks and
fair-weather patriots eye the pub's big screen. Salt
lauding over our wilted appetizers and
arteries alike as we pretend not to roil all night
with envy for those Olympian bones and
the way they glide in like beautiful cargoes.

## DEB NYSTROM

Deb Nystrom's most recent book of poetry is *Bad River Road* from Sarabande Books. A new collection, *Night Sky Frequencies,* will be out in 2016. Her work has appeared in *Best American Poetry, The New Yorker, Ploughshares,* and elsewhere. She teaches in the MFA program at the University of Virginia.

### When He Doesn't Come Home

I wait for the phone to ring, but I don't call nobody.
I wait in the dark, listening, or if I get up, I switch on lights, room to room.
    Somebody knew
I was scared, if they watched me looking in closets, closing curtains where
most nights they're left open. I hurry in the bathroom, then go back to the dark
    and listen, and I

think back through every room—*I could do without everything—now's the time, if*
   *I was*
*leaving,* I say to myself. The last night before they arrested him, it was getting
   light, and
I'd got so tired of wondering, I slid to the floor in the living room, saying *now*
*just straighten the fringe on the rug, concentrate on that,* so I'm listening, but for a
   while I
forget what for—takes a long time across one end, and then the other, and though
   I am
worrying, I'm not really thinking anymore, I'm getting every last string straight, no
tangles, each one parallel to the one beside it, and if some are shorter and some are
   longer,
I'll get the scissors when I stand up and go to the door to see what's there.

———————

## CLARE POLLARD

Clare Pollard has published four collections of poetry, the most recent of which,
*Changeling* (Bloodaxe Books, 2011), is a Poetry Book Society Recommendation.
Her play *The Weather* premiered at the Royal Court Theatre. She is currently
touring in a one-woman show based her latest book *Ovid's Heroines*, (Bloodaxe
Books, 2013).

### Boy Breaking Glass, Peckham

Boom!-*tunkle,* exploding easy, little man is
through glass-jaws, hooded, daylight raw:
it's war vs. the gang who check you, is
his crew innit, and the flatscreen TV Sonic
gonna take them places, fast. His CV is
shit, seriously; he's new-trainered, old-eyed.
The born-rich gawp at this filmed premiére.

## EMMETT, JIM, AND KAREN SHEPARD

Karen Shepard is the author of four novels, most recently *The Celestials*. She teaches at Williams College in Williamstown, Massachusetts, where she lives with her husband, three children, and three beagles. In addition to writing fiction, Emmett Shepard enjoys basketball and socializing. He published his first story in *Subtropics* while still an eighth grader, received the Edith Wharton Prize for Fiction as an eleventh grader, and is now a freshman at Pitzer College. Jim Shepard is the author of seven novels, including *The Book of Aron*, and four story collections, including *Like You'd Understand Anyway*, which was a finalist for the National Book Award and won the Story Prize. Five of his stories have been in the *Best American Short Stories* and two in the *PEN/O. Henry Prize Stories*. He teaches at Williams College.

### Vagrant

In our small yard in our
Small house, we are three, that beautiful,
Sturdy number. We clutch between us the flaw
That left the first one unborn and
Permanent in our terrible
Memories. With the lonely shine of ornament,
The first dangles over our
New tiny boy. His fist swats it like a barbarous
Chief dispatching his enemies, and
We touch the cold equivalent of metal
Against our forgetful hearts, while our little
Guru sees a vagrant, a brother, a man.

## DAVID WAGONER

David Wagoner has published twenty books of poems, most recently *After the Point of No Return* (Copper Canyon Press, 2112). His novel, *The Escape Artist*, was made into a movie by Francis Ford Coppola. A winner of the Lilly Prize, he was a chancellor of the Academy of American Poets for twenty-three years. He edited *Poetry Northwest* from 1966 to 2002, and he is professor emeritus of English at the University of Washington.

## That Boy Is Still Breaking Glass

That window was for nobody
but me, and nobody but me knew
what was on the other side or where
more light would be coming from till I
showed people where it was
and where it was going to be and,
look, that's plain as day now.
You can come and watch because I
showed just how good I am
at opening eyes and ears, no
matter if nights seem longer
and darker for you out there.

---

## JOHN COREY WHALEY

John Corey Whaley is the author of *Where Things Come Back*, winner of the
Printz and Morris Awards, and *Noggin*, a finalist for the National Book Award
for Young People's Literature. His third novel, *Highly Illogical Behavior*, was
published in 2016. Whaley lives and writes in Southern California.

## So There

On the shore where nobody
I know or will know or ever knew
Waves me out to sea where
We all get lost in the current and I
Can pretend I never was
And that I never saw and
Heard the way that now
Looks and sounds because I
Just am
Not here, no
I'm nowhere any longer
So there.

# A Bronzeville Mother Loiters in Mississippi. Meanwhile, a Mississippi Mother Burns Bacon

## TERRY BLACKHAWK

Terry Blackhawk founded Detroit's InsideOut Literary Arts Project in 1995. She is the author of *Escape Artist*, winner of the John Ciardi Prize; *The Light Between*; and four other collections of poetry. She won the 2010 Pablo Neruda Poetry Prize and is a 2013 Kresge Arts in Detroit Literary fellow.

### Tallahatchie

Peonies petal-shake in heavy
rain propped up by their companion-
able fence. Does structure help to
hold the deluge back? Let no scythe hack
a single sweet head down
nor wind a wire nor leave Chicago child unhorsed.
His memory is a river that
spreads mist still. Distant whistler, little
fall of bloom, droplets, eyes that saw no foe.

---

## KWAME DAWES

Kwame Dawes has published nineteen books of poetry. His latest collection is *City of Bones* (Northwestern University Press, 2016). He is Glenna Luschei Editor of *Prairie Schooner* and teaches at the University of Nebraska. He is director of the African Poetry Book Fund and artistic director of the Calabash International Literary Festival.

### Grown Up

I grew up the day sleep stopped promising magic. These
adult dreams are mere interruptions. When we were

children, we woke expecting new things. Now as grown-ups,
we wake with the deep groaning of memory. Grown-ups,

I've learned, can't forget the burnt bacon. As children, we were
in love with the soft oblivion of sleep. We supposed

that light would always come; it was our way to be
alive, to be giddy; such bliss before we grew old and wise.

---

## RAVEN HOGUE

> "Yazoo City" is a testament to my memory of my great-grandfather when I was
> child. I had heard tall tales about his strength, and I met him at his weakest.

## Yazoo City

Water bugs, beryl and brisk, were made of vinyl then.
Scratched the gospel in ochre under a
claw-footed tub. Great-grandfather's blood wilted in sickness.
He sucked his breath into a fist. The iron stove heaved
as they amputated his leg. Mercer churned within.

# Bronzeville Woman in a Red Hat

## LATASHA N. NEVADA DIGGS

LaTasha N. Nevada Diggs is the author of *TwERK* (Belladonna, 2013). Her interdisciplinary work has been featured at MoMA, the Walker Art Center, and the 2015 Venice Biennale. A native of Harlem, LaTasha is the recipient of numerous awards, including ones from the New York Foundation for the Arts and the National Endowment for the Arts.

### Cling

sapphires are lovely. the Star of Bombay most by Child.
she embodies its six rays replacing spoiled limbs. with
heat she hopes to change her lackluster, halt the continuing
spectrum an uncle sapped from her. a vampire's cling,
she remembers his as corn flower blue. a distracting issue
a lover is not guilty of. how does he know it's a turn off? *his*
dick cannot enter her that way nor retire to any position. No
moment to gaze without recall. shadows cannot swing or hang in
the amber bathroom light. she admires little if at all. a final
twinge as lover pinches when entering fearful pink-orange fire.

---

## EUGENE GLORIA

Eugene Gloria is the author of *My Favorite Warlord* (Penguin, 2012), *Hoodlum Birds* (Penguin, 2006), and *Drivers at the Short Time Motel* (Penguin, 2000). His honors include an Anisfield-Wolf Book Award, Pushcart Prize, and a National Poetry Series selection. His recent work appears in *The Best American Poetry 2014*, *TriQuarterly*, *Memorious*, *Prairie Schooner*, and *Ploughshares*.

### The Maid

Before she let her go not a speck of dirt
sullied her bleached blouse except for the dark

rope of hair she sometimes coiled into
a tidy bun with beaded sweat gracing the
mandarin collar and a pressed hanky the sun
lurking so the hanky became both veil and
rag unlike her skirt a bloomful
tent for tiny boys cooling with scent of sea air

Air rifling through the trees and
bloomful sheets with camisoles on the line
and the flag flutter warning of forbidden zones
sun scorching the grass into oaken fields
the yard where we hunted dragonflies well
into dinnertime or thereabouts until
dark I suppose or when rain fell—whatever
dirt or blemish upon her name only my mother knew

---

## MAXINE KUMIN

Maxine Kumin was the recipient of awards such as the Pulitzer Prize, the Ruth
Lilly Poetry Prize, the Robert Frost Medal, and most recently the 2011 Los
Angeles Times Book Award. She served as poet laureate of the United States
from 1981 to 1982, and taught at MIT, Princeton, and Columbia. Former poet
laureate of New Hampshire and former chancellor of the Academy of American
Poets, Kumin died on February 6, 2014.

### At the Capitol Hill Suites, 1985

When I asked for Gwen at the desk they
hesitated, said they only had
permission to provide her phone, never
divulge the room number. It was if I had
malevolent intent. She answered on Ring One.
Yes! Come up, come up, we'll change together in-
to our best clothes, we'll saunter to the
Poets Laureate event together, bring down the house,
take our bows before and after, after and before.

## STEPHANIE STRICKLAND

Stephanie Strickland has published eight books of printed poetry and ten works of trans-medial, digital poetry. Her awards include two Di Castagnola Prizes from the Poetry Society, the Sandeen and Brittingham Prizes, National Endowments for the Humanities and National Endowment for the Arts grants, and the Boston Review, Pushcart, and Best American Poetry prizes. stephaniestrickland.com.

### In a Red Hat

Golden cream it was Not.
Shovel black "it" was. Wise
Enough, full woman Enough
To, seated, withstand "*it*," To
Choose fire over Freeze,
To wear her red, robust Or
Rash or roaring warmth, Be
Pillar and pillow, not Afraid.
Fully conscious of the child, Conscious
Of care rapidly needed, conscious Of
Clinging. A, to her, necessary Kindness—
On her integrity looks Easy
But cannot be so, not for any Creature
Facing hatred, yet she made the Bond.

# The Chicago *Defender* Sends a Man to Little Rock

## SHARON DRAPER

Sharon M. Draper is the author of over thirty award-winning books, including *Out of My Mind*, which remains on the *New York Times* best seller list. She served as the National Teacher of the Year, has been honored at the White House six times, and has been a literary ambassador to Africa and China.

### Bleeding Brownish Boy

I fear for my ruddy-faced sons and grandsons, I
Know the pain of the past—it is not buried. I saw
Hatred spewed from the mouth of a gun, a
Smile forever frozen on a face. Bleeding, bleeding,
Like so many other mothers' bold, brash, brownish
Boys. The women have always feared for that boy.

---

## RITA WILLIAMS-GARCIA

Rita Williams-Garcia is the author of nine novels for young readers including the multi-award–winning *One Crazy Summer* series. She has been twice-named a National Book Award finalist and a Coretta Scott King Author Award recipient. Ms. Williams-Garcia is on faculty at the MFA program at Vermont College of Fine Arts.

### Meanwhile in the Henhouse

Her gate cracked open, complicit, she knew when
roosting hens' stir deafly heard as Beethoven
a straw movement. Truth tell it, is
no allegretto plucked but brutal
slashing over squawking vespers or

paws on a henhouse floor. Whispers
hush her raided site—yet all point to
its runny clue; a lady-like
gambol of no wings, flight. No air.

———————

## JAKE ADAM YORK

Jake Adam York was a poet and associate professor at University of Colorado,
Denver. His posthumous collection *Abide* (2014) was a finalist for the National
Books Critics Circle Award. York cofounded the journal *Copper Nickel* and was
a visiting faculty scholar at Emory University's James Weldon Johnson Institute
for the Study of Race and Difference and the Richard L. Thomas Professor of
Creative Writing at Kenyon College. York died in 2012.

## In Little Rock

Perhaps, this morning, we're there,
normal and soon forgotten, as news is
when it's passed over breakfast, like love,
something that's always cast, too
heavy to hold for long. We breathe it in,
the bacon, the coffee. We listen to the little
quavers as the local tongues, water over rock,
rise and fall, like stones skipping soft
into the white that smoothed them. The women
speak like grandmothers, softly
opening their mouths, opening
and drawing advice from themselves,
like biscuits, and offering in kindness
a little more than anyone could ask, more
than anyone can take. I know their pitying.
It looks like patience, the look on everyone's
faces as the peddler shuffles in his blindness,
black hand held open, everyone awaiting
the hiss of door, the whisper in everyone's
throats, breaking from patience into pleasure.

# The Chicago Picasso

## MAURA STANTON

Maura Stanton has published six books of poetry, most recently *Immortal Sofa* with the University of Illinois Press. She lives in Bloomington, Indiana.

### The Seahorse

The seahorse swims poorly but erect. Why does
it even try? It's always curling its tail around seaweed, like a man
who uses a cane to cross the street. Who could love
a swaying, wobbly creature like that? (Me!) There's an art
to swimming and the seahorse is worse at it than any man
who drives into Chicago and visits
the beach, then checks out the Chicago Picasso or the Art
Institute or the Aquarium. But
still I love to watch the seahorse trying hard as it swims and squirms.

## KEVIN STEIN

Kevin Stein has published eleven books, including his most recent collection of
poetry *Wrestling Li Po for the Remote* (Fifth Star Press, 2013), and the scholarly
work *Poetry's Afterlife: Verse in the Digital Age* (University of Michigan Press,
2010). He has also edited two important anthologies of Illinois poetry. He
succeeded Gwendolyn Brooks as Illinois poet laureate in 2003.

### Ars Poetica Composed While Dressing in the Dark

Up one sleeve my theory of poetry postulates a man
putting his shirt on backwards, how the world visits
arced backward around his sun-flecked neck like the art
of reversal epiphany rehearses in church—gods dead but
not—the way that collar's Easter gives him the squirms.

"Huh" means he's seen the unseen, a paradox of art
that cinches then frees like a button he can't reach hurts
the nobby cobblestone streeting his spine. That's art
unstitching seams, unraveling the slothful cloth. It urges
his shoulders forward, row-row-rowing inland voyages.

———————

## LIANE STRAUSS

Liane Strauss is the author of *Leaving Eden* (Salt, 2010); *Frankie, Alfredo* (Donut Press, 2009); and *All the Ways You Still Remind Me of the Moon* (Paekakariki Press, 2015). Her work is published widely in magazines on both sides of the Atlantic.

## Tender Visits

Because of who he is and what he does
in spite of what he says, what kind of man
he thinks himself to be, when he says *love,*
he means crusade. His holy land is Art.

Unlike that sculptor once, another kind of man,
suffering love's torments, who tendered tender visits
and turned to feeling life cold inert Art,
he seeks to halt and cool, to stay what but

for Art would burn, slip through, unfold. He squirms
when tears, or words, stream down, steers clear for Art.
It's Art he dreams, desires, until it hurts.

And so he turns to her the way he turns to Art,
tells her again he loves her, seems to, urges
her to undertake, with him, still finer voyages.

# The Children of the Poor

## SIOBHAN CAMPBELL

Siobhan Campbell is the award-winning author of several books including *Cross-Talk* (Seren) and *That Water Speaks in Tongues* (Templar). Widely published in journals including *Poetry, Hopkins Review, Asymptote, Magma,* and *Poetry Ireland,* Siobhan is on faculty at the Open University and works in post-conflict writing with veterans and others.

### The Climb

Addressing the mountain, we thought we knew its size and
had our maps, our compasses all synchronised when
down a cloud, fiercely opaque and wide
surrounded us, making our hopes vain, our world
its world for longer than we seemed able to count. Is
this what might construe a change of state or are we bitten
by dread of nature in the wild, the bitter physics of it, and
certain now of why we feel bereft, our mountain so bewarred?

––––––

## BRENDA CÁRDENAS

Brenda Cárdenas has authored *Boomerang* (2009) and *From the Tongues of Brick and Stone* (2005). She coedited *Between the Heart and the Land: Latina Poets in the Midwest* (2001). Her poems and essays have appeared or are forthcoming in *Poetry, Latina/o Poetics, The Wind Shifts, Pilgrimage,* and *Rattle,* among others.

### What Will We Give Our Children?

We shall give them tools—a golden shovel to dig a revolution of good food. What else but a Joe-Louis sized fistful of squiggles in their soiled palms? Yes, we shall hand them a hill of red worms, Walmart waste, brewery belch, and they'll say, "I grow my own lunch, raise my own supper—beets, greens, baskets of fish. I give

spinach to Sadie, milk to Maud, perch to the preacher, and the hunchback girl, my
sunny jar of honey harvested in our own Bronzeville." What to teach our children?
How about aquaponics and hoop houses? Seeding with the son of a sharecropper who
catches rain in food deserts, who feeds thousands on a few acres that are
climbing up to the inner-city sky like beanstalks? A golden egg for the poisoned poor,
how about a million pounds of groceries on zero fossil fuels? Big Agri-Corps who
alter genes, deplete nutrients, and truck Jack's beans from coast to coast are
stuffing us with wilted dreams and empty feasts. Why is Monsanto not adjudged
a toxic crime against humanity? Not redlined with the quick marts and the
box stores? Why not urge compost heaps to squat on vacant lots, or leastwise
herbs in pots on porches? This, so our cramped children might sprout tendrils of
curiosity, might learn to heat a house with a blanket of earth, to reach across the
table in the symbiotic grace of tilapia and coriander, to honor and share the land.

This farmer once shot hoops for the pros, did business for Colonel Sanders, but he
cashed in his retirement, risked it all for two acres and the next generation, leaned
his nearly seven-foot frame into broken windows and invention, across
color and culture, country and continent, yesterday and today for tomorrow:
"More greenhouses in the hood, less greenhouse gas in the air." Here, People
grow blue gill and bok choy, medicine and power, even community. He has said
that a log filled with spawn and sealed with wax will mushroom shitake ears, that
most of the world's farmers are women, and he'll pay them a living wage, that he
can put them to work in a garden all year long, that learning is evolution. His was
a spiritual revolution. But any people can cultivate their own sustenance by holding
tight to the glory of rhizomatic red worms and waste, to a bio-clean
future. What shall we give our children? No plastic earth, just the luminous globes
of their own eyes shining; just the bounty of their harvest and health; just in
time; just a forest-, olive-, avacado-, lime-, lettuce-, jade-green thumb; just his
Will Allen symbiotic grace of mind, heart, and the growing power of hands.

---

Lines by Gwendolyn Brooks, which run vertically down the right margin: from "The
Womanhood": "What shall I give my children? who are poor, who are adjudged the least-
wise of the land?" from "Medgar Evers": ". . . he / leaned across tomorrow: People said that
he was holding clean globes in his hands."

## KYLE DARGAN

Kyle Dargan in the author of *Honest Engine* and three other poetry collections from the University of Georgia Press. He directs the creative-writing MFA program at American University and edits *Post No Ills* magazine. He lives in Washington, DC.

### Sustenance

*Everybody needs beauty as well as bread, places to play in and pray in where nature may heal and give strength to body and soul.*

—*John Muir*

Were the choice mine—before beauty, what?—
I would beg bread or a pallet. For how shall
my eyes and ears digest grace while I
shiver, while anemia thins my blood? To give
is not to feed your own tastes. Understand my
hardship is not your canvas—invisible children
don't need beauty's mirrors to know who
stares back, gaunt. While it is true we are
souls, soul waits while growls the belly poor.

## REGINALD GIBBONS

Reginald Gibbons is the author of *Creatures of a Day* (finalist for National Book Award); *Slow Trains Overhead: Chicago Poems,* and *Stories; How Poems Think* (University of Chicago Press, 2015); and other books, including a novel, *Sweetbitter.* He is Frances Hooper Professor of Arts and Humanities at Northwestern University.

### A Neighborhood in Chicago

In its last halogen hours,
            the evening forgives the alley-

                        ways . . . wherein,
Every June morning, again,
            here are new leaves, viridian.

                        They'll come to.

They'll tremble toward the brightening.
        Instruments without musicians,
                they will play
A silence, soothing last night's
        bruised pianos and exhausted
                horns. For your
instruction, each meager leaf,
        shaped like, more intricate than, a
                violin,
accompanies rats and moths
        into the dawn, and a hiding
                cougar with
a wounded eye, a torn paw:
        in halogen night, no escape
                but by grace.

---

## LAURIE ANN GUERRERO

Poet laureate of Texas for 2016, Laurie Ann Guerrero is the author of *A Tongue in the Mouth of the Dying* (University of Notre Dame Press, 2013) and *A Crown for Gumecindo* (Aztlan Libre Press, 2015). She holds degrees from Smith College and Drew University and is the director of the Macondo Writers' Workshop in San Antonio.

## Play the Song

When I am gone, play the song. What
hum from boxes, play the song, from your small throats shall
unhinge the grief from your jaws, feed you more than I

ever could. Play the song when I can no longer give
beat, wrap my gray skin around ballad or blues. When my
hands, like leaves, shake themselves loose, my children,

when there is no more crescendoed mother, play the song, who
loved you, play the song. Play the song when all others are
filled with milk and money. Who can say that we were poor?

## JANICE N. HARRINGTON

Janice N. Harrington's *Even the Hollow My Body Made Is Gone* won the Kate Tufts Discovery Award. Her latest book is *The Hands of Strangers: Poems from the Nursing Home* (BOA, 2011). Her most recent book of poetry, *Primitive: The Art and Life of Horace H. Pippin*, appeared in 2016.

### Eve Wept

I cast you out into merciless lands, and neither guide nor
succor will you have. This is what you chose: grief.

Weigh, spend your coin of knowledge that is neither joy nor
lasting gain. But do not weep, beg mercy, plead love.

Do not petition for paradise. What *you* have willed shall
be done: get out. Wander naked on your wild earth and be

glad of the Serpent's gift. See how long it will prove enough.
I have made eternities. In each eternity, you are alone.

## RUTH ELLEN KOCHER

Ruth Ellen Kocher has published seven collections of poetry including, *3rd Voice* (Tupelo Press, 2016), *Ending in Planes* (Noemi Press, 2014), *Goodbye Lyric: The Gigans and Lovely Gun* (Sheep Meadow Press, 2014), and *domina Un/blued* (Tupelo Press, 2013), winner of the 2014 PEN/Open Book Award. She teaches at the University of Colorado.

### If Divorce Were Our Concerto

You play notes of white water or black water. They
are fingers or drapes, also. They pinpoint departure. Cascades perish
becoming not water but light. Not Christmas light. Light purely
mean and ruthless. I am pleading now. White is every illumination waving
goodbye. You utter a white scale of irises gone vulgar, brazen, their
stamen exposed like the black oboe, their inner sift and spill, spirits
left in a white circle of sheets. The bed, the room emptied, hence—

## SASHA PIMENTEL

Author of *Insides She Swallowed* (2011 American Book Award), Sasha Pimentel
has published in journals such as *APR* and *Crab Orchard Review* and was selected
by Philip Levine, Mark Strand, and Charles Wright as a finalist for the 2015
Rome Prize. She's an assistant professor at University of Texas El Paso.

### At the Lake's Shore, I sit with the sister, resting

Michael's skin splinters under the water's line, his navel and all murky and lost
like a city from my old life, or that scarf I'd loved, the softness
with which we sink into what disappears, and the country of his groin and knees
   so softly
already blackened. His sister snores beneath my hands; her mouth makes
tadpoles. Her breath wet from chemotherapy, I've massaged her a-
sleep. Her shoulders swell their small tides. The air burns leaves. I want to want to
   trap
her sighs dividing the stillness, in glass, to a jar—like smoke against a window—
   for
my lover, halved by water: but I've sat here before, in sun and grit, watched the
   waves which lose us.

## SHAZEA QURAISHI

Shazea Quraishi is a Pakistani-born Canadian poet, playwright, and translator
based in London, where she also teaches creative writing. Her collection *The Art
of Scratching* (Bloodaxe Books) was published in May 2015, and she is writing a
play based on her pamphlet *The Courtesans Reply* (Flipped Eye, 2012).

### The Inconditions of Love

Woken by a sound, a whimper-whine,
she sits up and the baby, whose
feet press against her huge, unridiculous

belly, wakens. *You heard it too? Something's lost
or hurt* . . . She gathers the blanket around her, its softness

a memory of her mother's voice, velvet rope softly
pulling her from deep sleep.
                    Night makes
her hungry. Stroking her belly she feels a
kick. That sound again. An animal in a trap.
    *Don't be scared. The night is for*
    *mercy, and dark to rest and comfort us.*

---

## DON SHARE

Don Share is the editor of *Poetry* magazine.

## On a Station of the L

Not wet black boughs at all, but people
who are scrambling, bewarred, who
are in no mood for your grown-ass velvet; who have
given their young mostly the prospect of living with no
plan, no penitence, just cool contraband: hard-bitten children
they take the L to school and make it home only if they can
be heard; only if they can be
hard.

---

## BRUCE SMITH

Bruce Smith is the author of six books of poems, most recently, *Devotions*, a
finalist for the National Book Award, the National Book Critics Circle Awards,
the LA Times Book Award, and the winner of the William Carlos Williams Prize.

"Cry, Baby" Garnet Mimms & the Enchanters sang & "The Sky is Crying"
sang Elmore James: Two of the songs that stop & frisk sorrow that
take the *rent-due, my baby left me* & wring the neck of sadness bystyle. They
are the crying blues [by Mr. Langston Hughes]. They are American. They are
the mouth around a vowel like a dog around a bone. They are quasi
religious. They are quasi profane. Who knows what's the contraband

& what's the lawful crossing into a new territory? The blues because
smuggled pleasure resembles pain, because it enchants, because it is unfinished.

---

## STEPHANIE LANE SUTTON

Stephanie Lane Sutton's poetry has appeared in *Thrush, Tinderbox, District Lit, elimae, Button Poetry,* and *Radius.* She is also known for her essays and performance work. She was a finalist in the Write Bloody Publishing New Author Competition and a semifinalist at the National Poetry Slam. Find her at stephanielanesutton.com.

### Women of the Poor

A man is working graveyard at the drugstore while
a woman is a fever. Coughs, bleeds, and sweats through
every cotton in the cold wood floors. Hips like gauze. A

mother calls that poison. But this one's throttling
like a radiator. Clouds brimming thunder. Dark
as a closed mouth. When a woman becomes a we

she looks for ways to unthread it. The others
look to bloom in the red fallow of her womb. Hear
that? It's the clink in her wine glass. The tongue of the

shoes in the closet, slowly lilting its steps to a little
chant. Each button on the housecoat lifting
its face out from its double-breasted helplessness.

---

## SPRING ULMER

Spring Ulmer is the author of *Benjamin's Spectacles,* winner of the First Book Award from Kore Press in 2007, and *The Age of Virtual Reproduction.*

## Slave Ship Captain's Great-great Granddaughter

I never wanted to become a white people
without a soul. A lone white person who
sleeps at night on the floor, neighbors yelling. I have
burnt my toast and the edges are no
treat, but I eat them, because even the children
I wrongly long to adopt wouldn't. I can
hear those motherless children throwing fits, be-
cause they're trying to be good, and it's hard.

———

## RONALD WALLACE

Ronald Wallace's twenty books and chapbooks include *For Dear Life* (University
of Pittsburgh Press) and *You Can't Be Serious* (Parallel Press), both published in
2015. Poetry series editor for the University of Wisconsin Press, he divides his
time between Madison and a forty-acre farm in Bear Valley, Wisconsin.

## Lost softness softly makes a trap for us

When we think of all the things in our lives we've lost—
Persons, places, things, and all the softness
That went with them—and we want, oh so softly,
To call them back from the hole that such loss makes,

Even memory, time's antagonist, cannot provide a
Hook, a lure, a snare, a tender trap
To keep them in, when all they want is for
Us to let them go, until there is no us.

# The Coora Flower

## JERICHO BROWN

Jericho Brown has published poems in *New Republic, The New Yorker*, and *The Best American Poetry*. His first book, *Please*, won the American Book Award, and his second book, *The New Testament*, won the Anisfield-Wolf Book Award. He is an associate professor at Emory University in Atlanta.

### Stay

All day, I kept still just to think of it—

Your body above mine, what was
A lack of air between us—hot but restful

As I sat center on my bed of learning,

Mouth open, memory touching nothing
That misses you when I stay quiet and un-necessary.

# Exhaust the Little Moment. Soon It Dies.

## KAREN VOLKMAN

Karen Volkman is the author of *Crash's Law, Spar, Nomina*, and *Whereso*. She
teaches poetry at the University of Montana.

### Two Collisions

Summer

Exposition: mountain-piece aflame, exhaust
attenuating down, the
arm is ash, a-dusting, little
limb, in that moment
the flick, the flak, sky-set, soon
west-woke, effulgent eye—it
gapes, inundates, illumines, dies.
Rises to rapacious rain and
obviates its declamation: Be
tear, be torn. Be it
in insuperable gash.

Winter

Sharp-shape, snow-shive, bitter splinter or
divagation in eye-gold,
descried. Eye it,
legitimate, in flecks: it will
fly. It will not
annihilate, not green sum nor spring come
in flouncing gowns again.
Kaleidoscopic berm in-
cising, this
collision—categorical, un-identical—
ash in an icy disguise.

# The Explorer

## ADRIAN MATEJKA

Adrian Matejka is the author of *The Devil's Garden* (Alice James, 2003) and
*Mixology* (Penguin, 2009). His third collection, *The Big Smoke* (Penguin,
2013), was awarded the Anisfield-Wolf Book Award and was a finalist for the
National Book Award and the Pulitzer Prize. He teaches at Indiana University in
Bloomington.

### The Explorer

I lied when Pops asked, but I'll admit it now. I did touch the blue egg to see if,
somehow,
it felt as much like the sky as it looked. The egg: speckled in its twiggy nest, eye
level to
8-year olds, perfect & off limits like the baoding balls on Pops' desk. Tom & I
tried to find
its mom, but the finches scattered when we came near. One twittered the alarm
from a
maple. Others balanced on wires, flapped their wings at us like we were gravity. I
can still
see how carefully Tom scooped the egg from the nest, then headed out to find a
spot
on the hazy March concrete to drop it. *I want to see if these things break into pieces
or in*
*half like on TV.* Always the follower, I followed him through the maples out into
the
the treeless street, my stomach dropping before the egg did. A crunch, then no
more noise.

# First Fight. Then Fiddle.

## LISA WILLIAMS

Lisa Williams is the author of three books of poems, including *Gazelle in the House* (New Issues, 2014). She is series editor for University Press of Kentucky New Poetry and Prose and teaches at Centre College.

### First Fight. Then Fiddle.

A poet is musician later. First
she must find the fight
that is hers, given music, thin silence. Then
as if handed a secondhand fiddle
with missing string, she can figure a ply
of her own, a ploy to play on the
tune from her instrument slipping
its frame—and needs not that prim string.

# Garbageman: The Man with the Orderly Mind

## FRANNY CHOI

Franny Choi is the author of *Floating, Brilliant, Gone* (Write Bloody Publishing),
a Rhode Island State Council on the Arts Fellow, a Project VOICE teaching
artist, and a member of the Dark Noise Collective.

## INSTRUCTIONS: Say it like it is.

but my mouth / uncorks cellars of light
when paperclip sentence structure / is not enough
which is always / which rises / the question / if
only words shot / straight sun-ward / the hands
of a child / whose only clockwork is / *let me in*
*let* / if only words / weren't iron / cardboard / clumsy
shoes / unbroken-in / could hold the frenzy
of a waterfall brain / always-new / don't say *flimsy*
or *fickle* of such rush / mouthful of every thought / whimsically
physical / blister over / lizard brain / if you dare / enlist

---

## OLIVER DE LA PAZ

Oliver de la Paz's latest book, *Post Subject: A Fable* was published by the
University of Akron Press. He teaches in the MFA program at Western
Washington University and in the Low-Residency MFA Rainer Writing
Program at Pacific Lutheran University.

## Blue Graffiti

On my neighborhood fences, once bare, now dilute
letters, sprayed in wide, bright strokes. Confusion
of line and scrimshaw on knotty cedar. A find
for any connoisseur of script. The names loom and
splay. Their frenzy makes my eyes explode

on the swell of their obstinate lines. How lovely our
fences now. How lovely the wave that breaks into mist.

---

## DENISE DUHAMEL

Denise Duhamel's most recent book of poetry *Blowout* (University of Pittsburgh
Press, 2013) was a finalist for the National Book Critics Circle Award. The
recipient of fellowships from the Guggenhiem Foundation and the National
Endowment for the Arts, Duhamel is a professor at Florida International
University in Miami.

## Recycling

We, who know it is
probably too late, do it anyway. Our light
bulbs (compact fluorescent) look enough
like pigs' tails to remind us (if
we'd forgotten) of our piggy-ness. Our hands
sort the glass from plastic, cardboard in
plastic (more plastic!) bins. Clumsy
is our language. "Green" is also the frenzy
of money, our false flimsy
innocence, and our camouflage, whimsically
patterned, calling us to enlist.

---

## DAVID GUTERSON

David Guterson is the author of ten books, including the novel *Snow Falling on
Cedars*.

## The Occasioned Contrition of a Cynic

Straightjacketed I'm bracketed. Is
that how it is? Such light
on the right, bright enough
to blind, fences me in. Hey, tool, when

trussed I'm amiss and this
bewilderment
sets in, I feel my lines crying,
I'm cruel to myself. No, I'll bull against
your edge or what the
rule is—why this? I mean, should dark
crudely dictate? The door shuts
when I work deep down
with a dull blade, and the
voice—mine—wears sightless mirrored shades.

———

## LLOYD SCHWARTZ

Lloyd Schwartz teaches in the University of Massachusetts, Boston's MFA
program, has published three poetry books, and edited collections of Elizabeth
Bishop's work. A Pulitzer Prize–winning critic, he reviews for NPR's Fresh Air.
His poems have appeared in *The New Yorker, Paris Review, Best American Poetry*,
and *Best of the Best American Poetry.*

### Is Light Enough?

Who's there? I can't seem to make out anything or anyone. Is
anyone there? Is that you? In this dim light
that's not light, it's not light enough
to see who's there. I've been waiting for you—asking myself when
you were going to come. Or call. I don't like this
uncertainty, this half-light, this state of bewilderment.
Make it stop. Make it stop before I start crying .
Now I'm shaking, shivering—I want to steady my head against
your chest. Where better to find peace? Wait! I hear your steps—the
sound of your breath, your breathing. Unmistakably yours even in the dark.
Come closer! Find your way into the room. The wind always shuts
the door, so you don't have to. Closer! Sit down
here, near me. Tell me something. Answer me. Is the
light enough? Should I tell you to open or pull down the shades?

## GRAEME SIMSION

Graeme Simsion is a novelist and screenwriter. He lives in Melbourne, Australia.

### Truth and the Garbageman

Into warm blood, truth is dilute,
The essence swirls in confusion.
Shelter our alchemy, help us find
The solutions with truth enough and,
Dear gods, protect, lest our substance explode.
Thick rain clouds brew beyond our
Shelter, dissolving into the mist.

As a point of difference, and in partial compensation for my limitations as a poet, the first words of each line are taken from Ms. Brooks's poem "Truth": viz "Into the shelter, the dear thick shelter"—a contrasting sentiment about our relationship with reality.

## MATTHEW ZAPRUDER

Matthew Zapruder is the author most recently of *Sun Bear*, 2014, and *Why Poetry*, 2016. An associate professor in the St. Mary's College of California MFA program and English Department, he is also editor at large at Wave Books. He lives in Oakland, California.

### Is Light Enough?

It never really occurred to me to ask Is
it and for what but I am glad she did for yes light
this morning through the open window is for once enough
to remind me being awake when
my wife is still safely asleep is sweet as this
life I have despite the bewilderment
of so many other failures like not feeling like crying
even a little when I walk past a man against
the wall of the museum on Third Street leaning the

deep red gash on his bare foot bleeds dark
music into my ears and his delusion shuts
a door when she wakes I will hold her hand and down
that road a little bit further we will travel toward the
time we will have forgotten we were not always shades

# Gay Chaps at the Bar

## SANDRA BEASLEY

Sandra Beasley is the author of three collections of poetry, most recently *Count the Waves* (W. W. Norton, 2015), as well as *Don't Kill the Birthday Girl: Tales from an Allergic Life* (Crown, 2011), a memoir and cultural history of food allergy. Her poem "Non-Commissioned (A Quartet)" won the 2016 C. P. Cavafy Prize from Poetry International. She lives in Washington, DC.

### Non-Commissioned (A Quartet)

I.

No will choose you. We
chose ourselves. What a man knew
in the concrete embrace of bunkers—how,
who—would never make it to
the foxhole. A sergeant catches the order
as it trickles down his just
commander's leg. We haul the
water. We lead the dash.
We're the vertebras necessary
so the skeleton can dance. We're the
18 rounds in the length
of a minute; the 50 pounds of
an M1928 haversack. We're the gayety
of five-card draw in
dead night, the muffled barter of good
smokes for bad booze. Privates taste
fear. A corporal will spit it out. Whether
a man remembers to thread the
diaper of his pack: the stuff of raillery,
except when it should
save your life. We chose to be
grenade men. There was no *slightly*.

There is no plum butter, no bread, no iced
tea, no lemon. There is a meat can. And
there may be meat in it. What's given
to a boy as he trembles, as he turns green,
is the lesson of swim or—
goddammit, swim. You serve or are served
on a stretcher. Once home, belly up
to the bar and speak of the hot
dusks—how you aimed the mortar—and
remember us, who stayed in the jungles lush.


II.


The difference between liver and
*foie gras*, we were taught, is in how we
hold a beast's head before feeding. We knew
the throat lining to be beautifully
calloused, like a palm. We learned how
to load the gavage, to
simmer corn in fat to give
their flesh fat in return. They told us to
keep the men. We discarded women
after hatching. The
smell was foul, but that's summer.

We could almost taste the spread,
rich in iron, surrendering to a tongue the
way an ice cube melts in the tropics.
Nothing was wasted. Of
the lies they'll tell, that's the worst: that our
care was a form of waste. It was love.

Everything stings less when
shot with whiskey. We took time to
pin tin to each swollen breast, to persist
even when they hollered or
the cage held more than it could hold.

We stroked their throats and called it a
sign of hunger
if they swallowed. We took off

shoes that shone with their filth. We knew
their feathers would not stay white.
No one had to give that speech,
nor show us how
their eyes would glaze when ready to
slaughter. How can I make
you understand? This was not a
form of betrayal. Look.
In the field, the officer's job is to make an
office. Anything else is an empty omen.

III.

But
nothing
ever
taught
us
to
be
islands.

IV.

If a mother cradles her son's face and
praises how *brave* he is, how *smart*,
how nimble or athletic,
she is teaching him the language
of easy victory—ten points scored for
his team, the test aced, the prick of this
needle to which he did not weep. An hour
in the trench offered what was

a different dictionary. We do not
speak of smart, or brave, or *honor in
battle.* That's for telegrams to the
parents, the posthumous curriculum.
Little sprinter, you have no
advantage in this marathon, no stout
legs to carry you to the finish line's lesson.
Those soldiers who showed
grace with a bayonet understood: how
the body must become a weapon to
be wielded; how every chat
is a conversation with
the self we want to save; how death
listens in, nodding. We
laughed at the lieutenants who brought
photos of sweethearts, because no
girl wants to kiss a mouth full of brass.
If the only volume is fortissimo,
it's not music that's playing. Among
all, what I recall is our
silences. Our greatest talents,
accomplishing with a look what to
a weaker man required a holler.
We raised them. We laid them down.
We learned faces but not the
names, and left lording to the lions.
The roof of the house I lived in
had a chevron's peak. I took in this
breath, then this. There was no other air.

## CM BURROUGHS

CM Burroughs is assistant professor of poetry at Columbia College Chicago.
She has been awarded fellowships from Yaddo, the MacDowell Colony, and
Cave Canem Foundation. Her poetry has appeared in journals including
*Callaloo, jubilat, Ploughshares, VOLT, Bat City Review,* and *Volta.* More
information available: www.cmburroughs.com.

## Stillborn [In Memory Of]

I lift the preserve and preservative hue. I call you goldenrod, jonquil, maize. When "citrine," when "aureolin," you shift at the opening. I drink from you, of you, to name you, to the name of you, your cenotaph etched with stones; my persist -ant thirst for what you would have been, so other than what you are; dear interior.

I am your mother, your stranger, your conjure woman; the film of you on my to- ngue. How you were lifted out, addressed, carried; how I expected I would hold you ~ thing that I had made. Plum. Then the heart-out pinkening secured in a arc in my arms. Everything they said would happen was happening—in hunger.

I taste you; I breathe as if needing to be beaten. Child—when they pulled you off.

---

## LAURA MULLEN

Laura Mullen is the author of seven books, most recently *Complicated Grief.* Her honors and awards include fellowships from the National Endowment for the Arts, the Rona Jaffe Foundation, and the MacDowell Colony. She is the McElveen Professor in English and director of creative writing at Louisiana State University.

## Amen

She caught the birth of cool, and saw its cost, knew
what it was to be so poor there wasn't anything to wear but white
ghosts: handed-down dignity, thin illusions, street-broken speech.
She caught the desperate pose and showed how
short a lyric life can be, lived as an image among images. To
those who would have told her what to see or say she said make
your own way, mine is the difficult: how we go on living in a
world we make up, frantic, from the scraps we're left . . .
Look To these rough edges, marks of anger, marks of hope: an
opening, be real and love, love, hold onto love as an omen.

## CHRISTINA PUGH

Christina Pugh is the author of *Perception* (Four Way Books, 2017) and three other books of poems including *Grains of the Voice* (Northwestern University Press, 2013). A 2015 Guggenheim fellow in poetry, she is a professor of English at the University of Illinois at Chicago and consulting editor for *Poetry*.

### Stand Your Ground

> *Seven years after Florida adopted its sweeping self-defense law,*
> *the shooting of Trayvon Martin, an unarmed black teenager,*
> *has put that law at the center of an increasingly angry debate*
> *over how he was killed and whether law enforcement officers*
> *have the authority to charge the man who killed him.*
> —Lizette Alvarez, New York Times, March 20, 2012

What crime could *Trayvon* stand for?
Some slender peregrination, youth-
inscribed, delivered him to woe is
*is*—to the sleeve that films the arm of a
law that fails to unbraid the frail
from the predator: derives a thing
singular, whitewashed, and never not
guilty, so let none of us be unafraid.

And while Trayvon's face reflects with
only lovely variant our president (the
syntax of his *dignitas*), some full-
blues' anguish-cry must justly jewel
from a people gut-tired of wile
gratuitous as gunshot; and sick of
scripts that flay a boy, that mighty
edict lit in irreverent rose-light.

## DANEZ SMITH

Danez Smith is the author of *[insert] boy* (YesYes Books, 2014) and *Don't Call Us Dead* (Graywolf Press, 2017). Danez is a 2014 Ruth Lilly Fellow and member of the Dark Noise Collective. Danez is from St. Paul, Minnesota.

## The 17 Year-Old & The Gay Bar

this gin heavy heaven, blessed ground to think *gay* & mean *we*
bless the fake ID & the bouncer who knew
this need to be needed, to belong, to know how
a man taste full on vodka & free of sin. I know not which god to pray to.
I look to Christ, I look to every mouth on the dance floor, I order
a whiskey coke, name it the blood of my new savior, He is Just
He begs me to dance, to marvel men with the dash
of hips I brought, he deems my mouth in some stranger's mouth necessary.
bless that man's mouth, the song we sway sloppy to, the beat, the bridge, the length
of his hand on my thigh & back & I know not which country I am of.
I want to live on his tongue, build a home of gospel & gayety
I want to raise a city behind his teeth for all boys of choirs & closets to refuge in
I want my new god to look at the Mecca I built him & call it damn good
or maybe I'm just tipsy & free for the first time, willing to worship anything I can
    taste.

## LEWIS TURCO

Lewis Turco is the author of *The Book of Forms: A Handbook of Poetics* and over fifty other books, a chapook, and monographs including, most recently, *The Hero Enkidu: An Epic*, published by Bordighera Press in 2015.

## Omen

They were not fools: our parents always knew
the mores, ways and words of all the white
folk that surrounded us. Even their speech
was not beyond us—it was not the *how*
that we found useless, but we were never to

become our "betters," we could never make
our skin turn white. We would always sing a
song that's black and blue; we'd always look
the way we look. We had to learn an an-
them of our own and follow our own omen.

# Jessie Mitchell's Mother

## JASWINDER BOLINA

Jaswinder Bolina is the author of *Phantom Camera*, winner of the 2012 Green Rose Prize in Poetry from New Issues Press, and *Carrier Wave*, winner of the 2006 Colorado Prize for Poetry. His latest collection, *The Tallest Building in America*, is a digital chapbook from floatingwolfquarterly.com. He teaches in the MFA program at the University of Miami.

## Jessie Mitchell's Father

| | |
|---|---|
| Ashes | *flowers* |
| might be | *were* |
| in the offing | *here* |
| and | *or* |
| near . . . | *there . . .* |
| He | *She* |
| subdued | *revived* |
| by an era | *for the moment* |
| unhinged | *settled* |
| or inundated | *and dried-up* |
| failings, | *triumphs,* |
| freely | *Forced* |
| reeking | *perfume* |
| from | *into* |
| fresh | *old* |
| gunmetal | *petals,* |
| thrust down | *pulled up* |
| a taut | *the droop,* |
| Diminished, | *Refueled* |
| Trounced, | *Triumphant* |
| sucked-up | *long-exhaled* |
| death. | *breaths.* |
| His | *Her* |

| coarse | *exquisite* |
|--------|-------------|
| black | *yellow* |
| dotage . . . | *youth* . . . |

------

## MIRIAM NASH

Miriam Nash is a poet and educator based in London. Her first chapbook, *Small Change*, is published by Flipped Eye. She won an Eric Gregory Award from the United Kingdom's Society of Authors in 2015 and was awarded a Fulbright Scholarship in 2012 to complete an MFA at Sarah Lawrence College.

### Greatgrandfather's Woods

Greatgrandfather's house is a house of guns. My
mother knows where the bilberries grow. Mother
knows spells to harebell stains, says *Eat, this is
Greatgrandfather's fruit*; we smash jelly
in fingers and shirts. My mother is hearted
and bound to these woods, harboured and
home again. Greatgrandfather's tongue she
keeps for these woods, her mouth has
a different name. A gun still breathes in a
copse nearby, Greatgrandfather's brain
in the birch. His house is a house of
antlers, preserves: confit, sauerkraut, jelly.

------

## UGOCHI NWAOGWUGWU

Ugochi Nwaogwugwu's one-woman show is a poetic multimedia experience. Her poems have been honored in the international anthology *A Storm between Two Fingers* and by notable organizations like Apples and Snakes in the UK. She is also an accomplished performer and has shared the stage with artists such as Common, John Legend, Femi Kuti, Seun Kuti, Queen Ifrica, Luciano, Shaggy, and many more. For more see ugochi.com.

## Split Personality

Ogechi walked to school juggling thoughts that made her head itch. Disturbed by
the daily comparisons.

Breathe. A black girl's pain is a private thing. Can't let them see she broken. Split
like ends, shattered

by the weight of false idols. Classmates' whispers whirl wind rubbish. Over-
processing banter like her

fresh hairdo. She felt anything but relaxed as she stared into the mirror. What was
really at the heart

of her altering the signature naija-threaded-style Mama would coif every morning
after she ate

a bowl of gaari and fried plantain? Snickering during lunch was overt. Gangs
would laugh at

the Nigerian princess. Chastise tailored African prints fresh from Aba she would
rock. Don't knock her

until you've traveled dusty roads in her snakeskin shoes. She straightens to fit in,
hacks away bulwarks.

# Kitchenette Building

## GREGORY DJANIKIAN

Gregory Djanikian has published six collections of poetry with Carnegie Mellon, the latest of which is *Dear Gravity* (2014). His poems have appeared in *American Poetry Review, Boulevard, Cortland Review, New Ohio Review, Poetry, Poetry Northwest, Southern Review*, among many others, and in over thirty-five anthologies and textbooks. He teaches at the University of Pennsylvania.

### Feather and Bone

The morning has grayed
like my mother's hair in
winter, like her hands, and
the little splash of gray
in her eyes. The morning is a dream
of birds for her, and makes
her pause at the window, a
little uncollected, to hear the giddy
sound of wings, a sound
of feather and bone rising not
singly, or out of weakness, but crucially, strong.

## PETER KAHN

Peter Kahn is a founding member of the London poetry collective—Malika's Kitchen. A high school teacher since 1994, Peter was a featured speaker at the National Council for Teachers of English annual convention. He founded the Spoken Word Education Programme at Goldsmiths–University of London and runs the program at Roosevelt University in Chicago.

## Gray

We crave the comfort of color, like leaves, like skin, like dirt. We
flutter our eyes, hankering for change's constant wheel. We are

the spin & rasp, the spokes & blur, the smoke & bellow. The things
hanging quietly in the garage. Hiding deep in the attic. What of

us? The coats, lost? What of the moments drowned in dust, dry
with creaking veins, cracked? Days languid & limp, leaking hours

like maple syrup-ing silently from decapitated trees? Months and
years tip-toeing, joining their marrow-tapped hands until the

decades bleed soot & ash, and loam begins its involuntary
freeze. What of those appled August afternoons we play-

ed in the backyard, the dog bounding about before his grayed
hide was put to sleep? Before tears dripped like November leaves in

piles you cannon-balled into with your little sister choking on giggles and
emerging red & yellowed long before the night of your hair ash-ed gray.

―――――――

## JOSÉ OLIVAREZ

José Olivarez is a poet from Calumet City, Illinois, and the program director at
Urban Word NYC. His first book, *Home Court*, is available at homecourtpoems.
tumblr.com/purchase. Follow him on twitter at @jayohessee.

## On My Eyelashes

Wake up. Still crusting my eyelashes—a dream
tangling itself in my hair. The word makes
knots of my dad's slowly graying beard, a
silver strand every time I say with giddy
craze: dream. Say: poetry. Say: teach. The sound
of shovels rooting and sun fanning backs, not

cash registers or calculator clicks. He hopes strong.
Underneath the graying exterior, he is tangled Like
gum and hair with thoughts of "no rent
due." Youth shadows his eyes. He knows feeding
on whims, nutritionless pursuits. Laboring to chase a
craze. He reached, too. He feeds his wife
now. Wants me debt free, balanced, up. Satisfying
him isn't easy. I rub my eyes, a
flake falls. Does that mean I'm a man?

---

## ALICIA OSTRIKER

Alicia Ostriker's most recent books of poems are *The Book of Seventy* and *The Old Woman, the Tulip, and the Dog*. Her most recent volume of criticism is *Dancing at the Devil's Party: Essays on Poetry, Politics, and the Erotic*. Ostriker has twice been a finalist for the National Book Award. She teaches in the Drew University Low-Residence MFA Program in Poetry.

### Dry Hours

Gwen, you are from Chicago and my family isn't, we
grew up in New York but all of us are
familiar with Depression. Remember the things
Roosevelt did for the country during the Great Depression of
the 1930's? The first hundred days in office was the dry
run for the New Deal. The Brain Trust spent eight hours
every day drafting policy. Relief, recovery and
reform: Glass-Steagall for the arrogant banks, jobs for the
jobless. Including artists. Later an involuntary
draft, when it came to war against Nazis, was the plan.
It worked, we won. The greyed-
out newsreels of the forties, the blackouts in
our cities, who can forget? And
you already were turning grey,
like Whitman after the Civil War wondering if the "dream"
was going to come true, or if capitalism makes

every dream finally turn sour, not to mention a
continuing harvest of strange fruit, mobs of wolves giddy
with the power of death. No sound
from the beaten bodies and not
a sound from the strong
oak limbs from which the bodies hung like
hams in a butcher shop. What was feeding
on those sights? Gwen, was there a
rush of sexual excitement a husband
felt? Was watching a lynching satisfying
to a
woman like to a man?

---

## MAYA PINDYCK

Maya Pindyck is a poet and visual artist living in Brooklyn, New York. She is the author of *Emoticoncert* (Four Way Books), *Friend among Stones* (New Rivers Press), and a chapbook, *Locket, Master* (Poetry Society of America).

### Close Memory

When the teacher lights yesterday's
cigarette, we line up to taste this garbage—
an early lesson for the wild children ripening
into wolves slamming lockers bolted in
the wall, flipping desks to break the
school's flat notes dropping in the hall.

---

## BARBARA JANE REYES

Barbara Jane Reyes is the author of *To Love as Aswang, Diwata*, which received the Global Filipino Literary Award for Poetry; *Poeta en San Francisco*, which received the James Laughlin Award of the Academy of American Poets; and *Gravities of Center*. She lives and works in the San Francisco Bay Area.

1.
We pray, and
We sing yesterdays
We left behind—garbage
We regret, naming, ripening—
We breathed in,
We daughters of the
Weeping in the hall

2.
We firebrand
We sang yes sister, days
We ran, garbed, waged
We wild, riled, opening
We let ourselves in—
We, surely the
We, we healed and held

---

## SASHA ROGELBERG

Sasha Rogelberg is from Charlotte, North Carolina, and currently attends Bryn
Mawr College.

### Who Has Given Us Life

When the parchment voices of my Bubbe and Zayde flutter
like the hesitant flame of their Havdalah candle or
my father muffs mistakes as he starts to sing
the *Shehecheyanu*, his favorite prayer, an
amendment occurs, turning wails of the Wall into an aria.
As my skepticism of religion, like a candle, softens down,
it's not God who convinces me of my ascension. These
familial croons are consecrated as they exodus the rooms.

## GEORGE SZIRTES

George Szirtes is a poet and translator. Born in Hungary in 1948, he published his first book of poems, *The Slant Door,* in 1979. It won the Faber Prize. He has published many since then, winning the T. S. Eliot Prize in 2004, a prize for which he has been twice shortlisted since.

### We are things of dry hours and the involuntary plan

Where are we now, where going? Who are we
from day to day, each night being the thing we are?
What have we woken from? Are dreams of such things
matters of morning and lunch and afternoon, or of
dry evenings, the mind growing ever more dry?

These are the days. These are the petty hours
we count between acts. This is the *here* and the *and*
that link our sentences, and this is the one *the*
we use just the once, our saying involuntary
as if it could be other, a purpose or a plan.

## ROBERT WRIGLEY

Robert Wrigley is the author of ten books of poems. In 1987, he and his wife, Kim Barnes, and their daughter, Jordan (who was still in the womb), had a lovely and fabulous dinner with Gwendolyn Brooks in Washington, DC.

### Even If We Were Willing

Residents of a many-roomed single edifice, we
know little of one another and think
we are individual beings, the very centers of
of the universe. About lives, we are lukewarm
to most not our own: they're molecules, we're water.
Seven billion is a number, but the one we hope
matters is ours, each one a life we cling to
in hopes of getting all we can get.
Number seven-billion-two-hundred's found his way in,
neither you nor me but deep in the sea of it.

# The Last Quatrain of the Ballad of Emmett Till

## CHRISTIAN CAMPBELL

Christian Campbell is a Trinidadian-Bahamian poet, scholar, and cultural critic. His widely acclaimed first book, *Running the Dusk* (Peepal Tree Press, 2010), won the Aldeburgh First Collection Prize and was a finalist for the Forward Prize for the Best First Collection, among many other awards.

### After the Burial: A Stanza

Hadiya's mother has someone else's eyes. She
fades behind the black glass, she kisses
the wind. The dark room of her
eyes is always damp—there the kids killed
time—the shoes, the majorette uniform, the boy-
friend letters, the carpet, the bed, and
the blank dolls. The other mothers sit where she
sits, singing their silence of the way it is,
the room of eyes, in black and white, forever unsaying sorry.

----

Hadiya Pendleton (1997–2013)

----

## MICHAEL COLLIER

Michael Collier's sixth book of poems is *An Individual History*. He teaches in the creative-writing program at the University of Maryland and is director of the Bread Loaf Writers' Conference.

### Len Bias, a Bouquet of Flowers, and Ms. Brooks

He arrives in the middle of her reading. She
has to stop and taking the flowers he's brought kisses
the beautiful young man whose yellow socks are her

doughty sweater's antithesis. What's said between them is killed
by applause, but not his smile, which is the smile of a boy
standing in the silence he's created, and
not her magnified stare, which says she
understands why he's arrived late, is
already leaving, and that he is sorry.

## MYRA SKLAREW

Myra Sklarew served as president of Yaddo Artists Community and as
professor of literature at American University. Her published books of poetry,
essays, fiction and nonfiction include *Lithuania: New and Selected Poems* and
forthcoming, *A Survivor Named Trauma: Holocaust and the Construction of
Memory.*

### Money, Mississippi 1955

Did the river cry to hold such a boy? Emmett's
hands at the bottom of the river. Emmett's mother
breathing at the top. Her tears. Is
the river swollen over its banks, holding a
nameless boy? A scot free killer, a pretty-face.
An innocent boy's whistle erased. A killed thing.

## PATRICIA SMITH

Patricia Smith is the author of seven books of poetry, including *Shoulda Been
Jimi Savannah*, winner of the Lenore Marshall Poetry Prize, and *Blood Dazzler*, a
finalist for the National Book Award. A 2014 Guggenheim fellow, she is widely
published and teaches for the City University of New York.

### Black, Poured Directly into the Wound

Prairie winds blaze through her tumbled belly, and Emmett's
red yesterdays refuse to rename her any kind of mother.
A pudge-cheeked otherwise, sugar whistler, her boy is

(through the fierce clenching mouth of her memory) a
grays and shadows child. *Listen.* Once she was pretty.
Windy hues goldened her skin. She was pert, brown-faced,
in every wide way the opposite of the raw, screeching thing
chaos has crafted. Now, threaded awkwardly, she tires of the
*sorries,* the *Lawd have mercies.* Grief's damnable tint
is everywhere, darkening days she is no longer aware of.
She is gospel revolving, repeatedly emptied of light, pulled
and caressed, cooed upon by strangers, offered pork and taffy.
Boys in the street stare at her, then avert their eyes, as if she
killed them all, shipped every one into the grips of Delta. She sits,
her chair carefully balanced on hell's edge, and pays for sanity in
kisses upon the conjured forehead of her son. Beginning with A,
she recites (*angry, away, awful*) the alphabet of a world gone red.
Coffee scorches her throat as church ladies drift about her room,
black garb sweating their hips, filling cups with tap water, drinking,
drinking in glimpses of her steep undoing. The absence of a black
roomful of boy is measured, again, again. In the clutches of coffee,
red-eyed, Mamie knows their well-meaning murmur. One says *She*
*a mama, still. Once you have a chile, you always a mama.* Kisses
in multitudes rain from their dusty Baptist mouths, drowning her.
*Sit still,* she thinks, *til they remember how your boy was killed.*
She remembers. Gush and implosion, crushed, slippery, not a boy.
Taffeta and hymnals all these women know, not a son lost and
pulled from the wretched and rumbling Tallahatchie. Mamie, she
of the hollowed womb, is nobody's mama anymore. She is
tinted echo, barren. Everything about her makes the sound sorry.
*The white man hands on her child, dangled eye, twanging chaos,*
things that she leans on, the only doors that open to let her in.
Faced with days and days of no him, she lets Chicago—windy,
pretty in the ways of the North—console her with its boorish grays.
A hug, more mourners and platters of fat meat. Will she make it through?
Is this how the face slap of sorrow changes the shape of a
mother? All the boys she sees now are laughing, drenched in red.
Emmett, in dreams, sings *I am gold.* He tells how dry it is, the prairie.

# The Life of Lincoln West

## HONOR MOORE

Honor Moore's most recent collection of poems is *Red Shoes*. She is also the author of *The Bishop's Daughter*, a memoir, which was a finalist for the National Book Critics Circle Award.

### Variation, the Birth of Lincoln West

Even at the start gate, each of us squeals
to the light, everything sudden, cold, and
his nibs the doctor steps back, plump
mother agog, as spank on the bottom,
it screams, will not remember this, looped
was the light, her face, its face down, up.
Apparent was entrance into place, but in
when? From where? And what says this ah,
the scream rising toward her? Her sleep scant,
blue-aproned, appears the receiving
nurse, infant creature in winding blanket
came: her new destiny, him now bending
into gurgle, giggle, tiny fists to
the world. How quickly this does pass!
Northeast of anywhere, a boy at the
end of a bench, grown but still her "bundle
of joy." Joy? She loosened him carefully:
The world had not welcomed her into
maternity, years of just them, the
warding off, the fright, all that waiting,
bearing she did with these mother-hands.
His mother, her hands: from all of that, this.

First and last words of my lines are lines 4–10 of Brooks's poem.

# A Light and Diplomatic Bird

## FIKAYO BALOGUN

Fikayo Balogun is a writer and spoken-word artist who studied Gwendolyn Brooks's works during her MA. She currently performs at poetry events and blogs at spiceplaza.wordpress.com. Fikayo dreams of publishing her own poetry collection, but in the meantime, she is working on a one-woman spoken-word show.

### Birdie

Pretty black flapping wings, a lost bird
wondering around searching for balance
thought too black, she gulped down bleach
now snow white, a bleached black she does make
something carved, truly lost, she is a white miniature.

----

## TRACI BRIMHALL

Traci Brimhall is the author of *Our Lady of the Ruin* (W. W. Norton), winner of the 2011 Barnard Women Poets Prize, and *Rookery* (Southern Illinois University Press), winner of the 2009 Crab Orchard Series in Poetry First Book Award.

### Humbug Epithalamium

Let's put down our swords, my six-fingered jester. Oh
sweet and profane kisser, let's cap our poison, open
our hymnals and spend our last virgin hours apostolic,
fevered, undeceived. I've fallen for you from every height,
and they all bring me here—on bruised knees and
saying not yet, and yes, but not until you blush and tell
me only God watches, and he's shy. My Sin-eater, my

Master, salute or warn me but make it soon. My Humbug
Prince, you charm the robe off of Mary. Teach me how
to un-blue myself, to riot, to pin a boutonnière, to
spread the bed sheets on the pew. Sing. Linger. Start.

---

## STEPHEN DUNN

Stephen Dunn is the author of eighteen books of poems, including the recent
*Keeper of Limits: The Mrs. Cavendish Poems* (Sarabande) and *Lines of Defense*
(Norton). He was awarded the Pulitzer Prize and is the recipient of many other
prizes. He lives in Frostburg, Maryland.

### I Do Not Want to Be

I do not want to be
light and diplomatic man, quick
to forgive his nation's sins. The dilemma
remains. A singular act of
significance is difficult the
more one is of two minds. I watch the leaves
fall in the fall. Nothing discloses
the way I feel more vividly than the twists
of a few reddish ones in the breeze, and
is that why I'm so quiet here? Tact,
I fear that may be the cause. I'd like to
be able to scream, make a scene make me.

---

## LEONTIA FLYNN

Leontia Flynn has published three poetry collections with Jonathan Cape and
has received the Forward Prize for Best First Collection, the Rooney Prize,
the Lawrence O'Shaughnessy Prize for Irish Literature, and the AWB Vincent
American Ireland Fund Literary Award. She was born in 1974 and lives in
Belfast, where she is research fellow at the Seamus Heaney Centre for Poetry.

## 1982

At the last stop before town we all alight:
my sisters—the eldest, second eldest—and
lagging, chattering, nervously diplomatic
me running between them like a little bird.
At the bend where the tallish, balding Scots pine is
*Oh evening breeze*, it sways, *be easy, lenient!*—
we pass by the cattle grating and go in.
the kitchen works its dark, food-smelling alchemy;
the radio bleats. My mother, at the window,
is its light, its nesting-bird, its rooted tree.

---

## NIKKI GRIMES

Nikki Grimes is the recipient of the 2006 National Council for Teachers of English Award for Excellence in Poetry for Children. Her works include *Meet Danitra Brown;* American Library Association Notable Book *What is Goodbye?;* Coretta Scott King Award–winner *Bronx Masquerade;* and Coretta Scott King Author Honor books *Jazmin's Notebook, Talkin' about Bessie, Dark Sons, The Road to Paris,* and *Words with Wings.*

## Storm

Yesterday, God skipped thunder like stones, lashed
the land with pellets of H20, each illumined with
scissored bits of lightning—a riot
of sight and sound, sharp as red
sudden as death. Watch for grayed skies and
grief remembered. Both, for a moment, paint the world black.

---

## DOROTHEA LASKY

Dorothea Lasky is the author of four books, most recently *Rome* (Liveright/ W. W. Norton). She is an assistant professor of poetry at Columbia University's School of the Arts and lives in New York City.

## A Final and Unrepentant, Silent, Sorry Bird

Look at the green and yellow feathered, large-headed Bird
There in the room, on the burning ring of jewels he finds his balance
Oh I am so glad I did not find him in the kitchen, with the bleach
Then a greater doom, a final croak, not love, we would surely make
As it is in all awakening that what you want and love is made miniature

---

## LISA GLUSKIN STONESTREET

Lisa Gluskin Stonestreet's *The Greenhouse*, winner of the Frost Place Prize, was published by Bull City Press in 2014, and *Tulips, Water, Ash* was awarded the 2009 Morse Poetry Prize. Recent poems have appeared in *Rhino, Zyzzyva, Blackbird, Collagist,* and *Kenyon Review Online.* She writes, edits, and teaches in Oakland, California. lisagluskinstonestreet.com.

## the little-known bird of the inner eye

regal in its flecked-gold field, bird-
body of flake and vellum. Balance
on its branch, bleach-
white bones open to air. Make
of it what you will. Conduit, cave. Miniature

way-in, channel, funnel, small Valhalla
in its brick-red gaze. Hallway of *in*, of *of.*
Byzantine twist of *my*,
hollow of *eye* at its unblinking heart.

---

## TERESE SVOBODA

Terese Svoboda is the author of six books of poetry, the most recent *When the Next Big War Blows Down the Valley: Selected and New Poems* (Anhinga Press, 2015). Her biography, *Anything That Burns You: A Portrait of Lola Ridge, Radical Poet* appeared in 2016.

## Bird Boy

He—
I am the one to notice—squats behind the can
riotous with trash, and sings without abash-
ment, as if his
                wants were laid upon the lid, a barmecide
to passersby, imaginary feast, and we appreciate it. We—the
            sidewalk-blind—progress as fantoccini,
                        our strings flying, our legs of
wood clattering, *hup to*, his
begging discomfiting, until we—myself, at least—rush out of
range.

---

## TANA JEAN WELCH

Tana Jean Welch is the author of *Latest Volcano*, winner of the 2015 Marsh Hawk
Press Poetry Prize. Her poems have appeared in journals including *Southern
Review*, *Gettysburg Review*, *Beloit Poetry Journal*, *Prairie Schooner*, and the
anthology *Best New Poets*. Born and raised in Fresno, California, she currently
lives in Madison, Wisconsin.

### Sanctuary

She looks at her bruises in the window and

                        cannot tell
    the difference between her father and herself. Does my
father's anger go deeper than this? Is his abuse my humbug?

    Or can I be like the tufted titmouse who learns how
                to evade the hawk, comes to
            love despite the hovering threats? To start

            at fourteen-years-old and to know the bird
is blown in either direction. But the titmouse makes balance
    look easy—from electric wire to rail to the bleach

bottle. Watching the gray bird make
its leaps she comes to her mother hanging the miniature
houses from the back awning. Out this window—a tiny Valhalla

for chickadees and wrens, a place for her mother outside of
her beaten body. Gray bird, she whispers, mark my
skin, huddle my heart.

---

## JANE YOLEN

Jane Yolen is the author of over 350 books for children and adults. She was
recently given the New England Public Radio's Arts and Humanities Award,
the first writer to be so honored. Her adult poetry books include *Among Angels*,
(Harcourt), *The Radiation Sonnets* (Algonquin), *The Bloody Tide* (HolyCow!
Press), and five other collections.

### Solitaire

A single solitaire, that thrushlike bird
keeps its bank balance
fruitful in those bushes that never bleach
in winter's wind. Juniper can sure make
the magnificent out of the miniature.

# A Lovely Love

NICOLE COOLEY

Nicole Cooley is the author of five books, most recently *Breach* (Louisiana State University Press) and *Milk Dress* (Alice James Books), both published in 2010. She is the director of the MFA program at Queens College–City University of New York and lives outside of New York City with her husband and two daughters.

## Of Marriage: River, Lake and Vein

We have to go back to that shoreline, that coast where
we swam in flood water, not the hospital bed where you

lay alone, body twined in sheets. River where we've
sat together, silence a loose rope between us, river where we've thrown

rocks in the shallows, in the flat mud, river where you have asked me
not to talk about future. Follow me to that beach, scraped

and raked clean. No shells, no fish, twigs or branches. Tell me
how we will live now, how we will learn to live with

threat. The ruined is not a world of your
devising. All I want is your body on mine. Your kiss,

your breath on my neck. At the edge of the river, all we have
is this world we've made, is this world of two we have honed,

This world, dredged and flooded. Tell me
how much longer to wait? How to sit in the half

light of late afternoon, by the barge sunk in mud, released
from its motion. Will you follow me,

—or not—into the After?
I'm looking for you in the emptiness, in this—

---

## REBECCA HAZELTON

Rebecca Hazelton is the author of *Fair Copy* (Ohio State University Press, 2012) and *Vow*, (Cleveland State University Press, 2013.) Her poems have appeared in *AGNI, Southern Review, Boston Review, Best New Poets 2011,* and *Best American Poetry 2013* and *Best American Poetry 2015.* In 2014, she won a Pushcart Prize.

### House with an X on the Door

It might mean *pass over,* it might mean *sick,* and
yet whether the faint strains are pathogen or *Dvořák* played
on a continuous loop. the result's the same: we
cross ourselves, too, and walk on, having found
it's easier to assume an apple bruised is flush with rot.
So the house we dread is the house we make.
But were I on the inside, walled up with you, I'd forget the
vectors, drop my mask and sour perfume, breathe petals
cool against your lips till both fever and walls fall.

---

## COLLEEN MCELROY

Colleen J. McElroy, professor emeritus at the University of Washington, has published nine collections of poems. Her latest collection, *Blood Memory*, was published by the University of Pittsburgh Press in 2016.

### Throwing Stones at the All White Pool

the first plopped mid-pool leaving an oh-so shallow cavern
the second closer to shore rippled in eddies of kindness
after that they all joined in willy-nilly they all silly smiled
as we eased toes in refused to show hurt that never goes away
we owned the pain   broke the barricades   owned up to our
small failures   eight year old bodies prickled with icy shocks

# The Lovers of the Poor

## NATHANIEL BELLOWS

Nathaniel Bellows is the author of the poetry collection *Why Speak?* (W. W. Norton) and the novels *On This Day* (HarperCollins) and *Nan* (Harmon Blunt Publishers). He lives in New York City.

### A Legacy

In their day, the house was full—filled with finds from Their
travels, a vast collection, later broken, later sold; this League
of two, the wandered world, the young left all alone. Little is
or would be left: a bowl, a note, two blue-gray eyes; allotting
prizes was not her gift, nor any kind of kindness; her largesse
a mix: imperiousness, wit, a body knit from exhaust. Now to
take stock: unknown bronzed figure in a velvet box; dust, the
residue of want—peace in the place of all that has been Lost.

---

## ALISON HAWTHORNE DEMING

Alison Hawthorn Deming is the author of five books of poetry including most
recently *Stairway to Heaven* (Penguin, 2016). Her most recent prose work is
*Zoologies: On Animals and the Human Spirit* (Milkweed, 2014). She is Agnes
Nelms Haury Chair of Environment and Social Justice at University of Arizona
and a 2015 Guggenheim fellow.

### Cartoon

I found an old cartoon my brother drew, our mother keeping
the folded yellow second sheets, their
pencil lines smudged, with other items scented
like sawdust and lead, marked *Mementoes which mean a great to me*, bodies
for both of them now things of the past in
which they no longer labor or love or linger over the

details of family history as I do trying to center
myself in their absence and love them without taint of
anger or judgment or regret, just carry the
sense of them a little further down the hall
that leads away from the rooms in which they died as
if the cartoon might be what they
need in the afterlife I'm making for them in this walk
down the page. Hello, my brother, come down
to me from heaven or up from hell, the .
difference is nothing but a hysterical
joke once you've drawn your dark version of a pool-hall
Christ, *Joe and Mary*, hot rodding toward Bethlehem—they
look in vain at motel and bar and *Dirty Eddie's Gas* for someone to allow
them refuge—*and Mary was eight months gone*. Their
flight from *Governor Graft* must say something lovely
about you as a teenager wounded into darkness, a boy who skirts
the edge of disaster by replacing *Gov. Graft* with *Dirty Eddie* (to
note here same toothy grin of greed on both, cigar in teeth, men who graze
on poison and make a deal the desperate can't refuse). No
story our mother believed, the nativity, but art might mean you'd make it over the
   wall.

---------

## NATHAN HOKS

Nathan Hoks is the author of two books of poetry, *Reveilles* and *The Narrow Circle*, which was a winner of the 2012 National Poetry Series and published by Penguin. He is an editor and letterpress printer for Convulsive Editions and teaches in the University of Chicago's Committee on Creative Writing.

### The Empathy Nest

I need an emotion of tin,
A malleable nest I can
Bend, crumple, or use to block
The child's eyes, their invisible fire

That consumes the itch to escape.
They are a stew of chitterling.
They clip my mental swagger,
Sizzle and probe my eyes seeking

What? Not sympathy. This youth
Isn't a poster smattering and
Lulling the lot of unpuzzled
Cynics. This son's the wreckage

Of my sun, my peaceful middle,
Blossoming ghostly passage
Of screams and blood and urine,
My secret smeary mirror of stale

Off-white civilian shames.
Snow falls, streets slicken, and again
The apathetic eat gold porridges.
My tin droops, so underslung,

About to touch the ground and children,
(The crawling hordes of children,
Mine or another's horde of children?)
That grief may at least destroy all heavens.

----

## AMY LEMMON

Amy Lemmon is the author of the poetry collections *Fine Motor* and *Saint Nobody* and coauthor, with Denise Duhamel, of *ABBA: The Poems* and *Enjoy Hot or Iced: Poems in Conversation and a Conversation*. She is professor of English at the Fashion Institute of Technology–State University of New York in New York City.

## Logistics for Thursday

Here's the deal: I'll buy
the first round of drinks, you cover the
appetizers and we'll go from there. Right
from the get-go we'll exchange books
and furtive, searching glances. All in
fun, of course—it's not as if the
future depends on any one evening, our best
behavior or the glue of a slim volume's bindings.
Is that your hand on my back as we saunter
to the park along the river? "Go on,"
I say, as you talk about the woods in Michigan
and I tell you again about Ohio at Easter,
all the green, the flowering trees, mornings
starting later than here on the coast. In
the middle of a sentence about the timing of sun-
rises and sunsets, you'll stop me with a kiss—Yes!—or
maybe my words will just be swallowed by the wind.

––––––––––

## RACHEL MCKIBBENS

Rachel McKibbens is a two-time New York Foundation for the Arts poetry
fellow and the author of *Pink Elephant* (2009), *Into the Dark and Emptying Field*
(2013), and the chapbook *Mammoth* (2014).

## Black Friday

Everyone in the classroom knew whose
blood it was in the hallway. If a father trains
his son to roar and clank,
what can be done with a coming out?
We watched a lone tooth sail across
the room, then the mother rushed, picked up her
pearls and wilted son: ripped shirt, swollen
eyed. She left, holding him to her chest, a second heart.

## GREGORY PARDLO

Gregory Pardlo's collection *Digest* won the 2015 Pulitzer Prize for Poetry and is a finalist for the Hurston-Wright Legacy Award. His other honors include fellowships from the National Endowment for the Arts and the New York Foundation for the Arts; his first collection *Totem* was selected for the APR/ Honickman Prize.

## The Wedding Planners

We need a preacher who'll say *up in here* instead of *herein.*
Our vows should reference calla lilies and the snowy pistils they
jab ardently at our faces. Let's place their linty, foul-mouthed kiss
at the center of satin table cloths white as bee-boxes and
us buzzing like the ichthyic insects we'll invent: "coddle-
fish" finning the air, murmuring for words beyond *Civil* and
*ceremony*, beyond moderation, all our senses under assault.

## LEAH UMANSKY

Leah Umansky is a poet and teacher in New York City. She is the author of the *Mad-Men* inspired chapbook, *Don Dreams and I Dream* (Kattywompus Press, 2014) and the full-length collection, *Domestic Uncertainties* (BlazeVOX, 2013). Her poems can be seen in *Poetry, Barrow Street*, and *The Brooklyn Rail.* http:// leahumansky.com.

## The Left-Hour

In the left-hour, that vanished moan of a something,
the dark seems closed and closing-still. (What is it called,
when the last blink of a dream sends out its best chitter
                                    and its sorest lings?)
Tell me. I must know if this search is in stages or if the
search will end? Will the muscle, musk & bone of darkness
hold its trot, or force my musket-heart to recoil and draw?

# A Man of the Middle Class

## ELISE PASCHEN

Elise Paschen's most recent poetry collection is *The Nightlife* (Red Hen Press, 2017). Her other books include *Bestiary and Infidelities* (winner of the Nicholas Roerich Poetry Prize). Her poems have been published in numerous anthologies and magazines, including *The New Yorker* and *Poetry*. She teaches in the MFA writing program at the school of the Art Institute of Chicago.

### Division Street

The spire of Holy Name Cathedral rose like a prayer
above Chicago Avenue. I thumbed a leather-bound book
in catechism class, recited the *Hail Mary*. Fire and
devils blazed at night. The nuns told my mother
I had a calling. On Scott Street a man lay shot
dead in our alley. It was the Gold Coast. They prided themselves
on sidewalks safe as shrines. I questioned God, the last
to leave the room. Riots flared in Cabrini Green that Sunday.

---

## TRACY K. SMITH

Tracy K. Smith is the author, most recently, of the memoir *Ordinary Light*.

### Semi-Splendid

You flinch. Something flickers, not fleeing your face. My
Heart hammers at the ceiling, telling my tongue
To turn it down. Too late. The something climbs, leaps, is
Falling now across us like the prank of an icy, brainy
Lord. I chose the wrong word. I am wrong for not choosing
Merely to smile, to pull you toward me and away from
What you think of as that other me, who wanders lost among. . . .
Among whom? The many? The rare? I wish you didn't care.

I watch you watching her. Her very shadow is a rage
That trashes the rooms of your eyes. Do you claim surprise
At what she wants, the poor girl, pelted with despair,
Who flits from grief to grief? Isn't it you she seeks? And
If you blame her, know that she blames you for choosing
Not her, but me. Love is never fair. But do we—should we—care?

# Mentors

## SHARON OLDS

The twelve collections published by poet Sharon Olds include *Satan Says* (1980), *The Dead and the Living* (1984), *The Wellspring* (1996), and *Stag's Leap* (2013), which won both the Pulitzer and T. S. Eliot Prizes. Olds was New York State poet laureate from 1998 to 2000 and is currently a professor at New York University.

### Golden Nosegay

Dear Miss Brooks, this is another nosegay For
*for I am rightful fellow*. Whenever I
saw you, I gave you a small bouquet, am
in your debt kneel-deep for your *rightful*
*fellow,* each of us a girl fellow
of the men and women who sang in front of
and before us. What you claim for their
band, I would claim—to be rightful fellow of your band.

---

## BARON WORMSER

Baron Wormser is the author/coauthor of fourteen books. His most recent book of poetry is *Unidentified Sighing Objects* published by CavanKerry Press. He has received fellowships from the John Simon Guggenheim Memorial Foundation and the National Endowment for the Arts. He teaches in the Fairfield University MFA program.

### Sentence

Easy to wake, enjoy this day where someone named "I"
Goes forth to smell flowers, drive a car, swear
At some small annoyance while wondering how to
Hold this day not just in present-tense focus but keep

The past of it there, the grit in history's pipes, the
Fear beneath the bed and school and office where the dead
Can be heard faintly rattling bones, spitting upon
The presumptions of persons who think (or wish) that my
Life has no shadows, who say to death Never Mind.

# The Mother

## JEHANNE DUBROW

Jehanne Dubrow is the author of five poetry collections, including most recently *The Arranged Marriage, Red Army Red*, and *Stateside*. She is the director of the Rose O'Neill Literary House and an associate professor of creative writing at Washington College, where she edits the national literary journal *Cherry Tree*.

### My Mother Speaks to Her Daughter, Not Yet Born

Conceive of me before you—and believe / me, mija, there was indeed before. That *me* / wrapped masa in plaintain leaves. Or I / was esposa, occasionally mujer who knew / a tea for bringing children. I thought of you / the way women think of travel. And though / I once chewed coca leaves in the Andes, faintly / sick with altitude, the road stayed blurred and / distant. I thought of you like water as I / walked through cloud forests, ferns I loved / tendrilling with dew. The chocolate that I / drank was dark with you, a heat I loved / for its cinnamon. The market-place was you. / The beans in wooden bins. The loom. You were today and all.

---

## RACHEL CONTRENI FLYNN

Rachel Contreni Flynn is the author of *Tongue* (Red Hen Press), *Ice, Mouth, Song* (Tupelo Press), and *Haywire* (Bright Hill Press). She teaches at Colby College and is on the editorial board of the *Beloit Poetry Journal*.

### Daughter-Mother

A certain mother left me. And I believe
she no longer exists, no longer leaves me.

She does not slap and shriek at breakfast, *I
never wanted this*. Even then I saw and knew

that certain mother. You, your sadness. Now you

are like my daughter, child-like, in pain though
you don't admit such weakness. But I hear, faintly

at dawn, my daughter-mother needing sustenance and
of course I go. There is nothing better that I

could do to prove that I exist and am, after all, loved
than to rise and go forth, though for certain I

harbor shrieking, and may never admit I loved
even those crazy breakfasts, your sadness, you.

––––––––––

## ADAM M. LEVIN

Adam M. Levin is a writer from River Forest, Illinois. He's a founding member
of the University of Wisconsin's First Wave Learning Community and Young
Chicago Authors' Teaching Artist Corps, as well as the founder of Young Chicago
Authors' Emcee Wreckshop program. He's a full-time spoken-word educator in
the Chicagoland area.

### We were gonna go through with it, and then we lost it.

You are one of three people who know. I
didn't want to get anyone's hopes up—if people knew
that's when shit goes wrong. But it did, so now you
know. Man, I love this girl so much. I do. Even though
she puts me through so much shit, man. Sometimes, faintly,

I hear the second heartbeat again. (Remember you don't know this, and
if you tell anyone, we're never speaking anymore. Ever.) I
wait until she's asleep and pull out the paper with baby names we loved,
and read over them and they run together and I
start crying. You would've been a godfather. You would've loved

being someone's godfather. Imagine something so much smaller than you
so large once it's in your arms. Then it's gone. But the love never is. At all.

## GAIL MAZUR

Gail Mazur's books include *Forbidden City*, (University of Chicago Press); *Figures in Landscape; Zeppo's First Wife: New and Selected Poems*, winner of the Massachusetts Book Award, finalist for the Los Angeles Times Book Prize; and *They Can't Take That away from Me*, finalist for the National Book Award.

### Believe That Even in My Deliberateness I Was Not Deliberate

We'd be calm, we'd be serene, as long as we could believe
in the blue dragonflies and balletic monarchs that
hovered near us in a kind of peaceable kingdom even
while my love's illness menaced the peace in
the summer yard, in the fragile house, in the air I breathed in my
deliberateness. My only stratagem, deliberateness:
to accept our lot in that pathless time. I
thought I'd know what he'd want; what I'd want was-
n't any different. Wouldn't it be, wouldn't it finally be, not
to consider how finite our August? Not to deliberate?

## PATRICIA MCCARTHY

Patricia McCarthy is the editor of *Agenda Poetry Journal* (www.agendapoetry. co.uk), and won the National Poetry Competition in 2013. Her work has been published widely and anthologized. Her latest collections are *Rodin's Shadow* (Clutag Press/Agenda Editions, 2012), *Horses between Our Legs* (Agenda Editions, 2014), and *Letters to Akhmatova* (Waterloo Press/Agenda Editions, 2015).

### Childless Woman

Other people's offspring are hard to take; you
see them as miracles you never performed, try not to remember
the ones you lost from your womb: girls with the
intense look of yours in their eyes, at play with other children
in sand pits, on roller skates, pink ribbons in their ponytails. You
dress them in hand-smocked tana lawn frocks, pretend they got

double firsts just for being themselves. The fortune teller says that
three boys, not girls, are looking out for you up there. You
imagine them heartbreakers delivered by a stork. Even if you did
shy away from hushabyes once, now you would not.
Too old to carnival into motherhood, poems are all you can beget.

_____

## PAULA MEEHAN

Paula Meehan was born in Dublin, Ireland. She has published six award-winning
collections of poetry including *Dharmakaya* and *Painting Rain*. In 1915 she
received the Lawrence O'Shaughnessy Award for Irish Poetry and was inducted
into the Hennessy Literary Hall of Fame. She is Ireland Professor of Poetry,
2013–2016.

## The Ghost Song

From a dream of summer, of absinthe,
I woke to winter. Carol singers
decked the walls of some long lost homeland,
late night shoppers and drowsy workers
headed for the train.
                    So the night that
you died was two faced: June light never
far from mind though snow fell. I handled
grief like molten sunshine, learned to breathe
your high lithe ghost song from thinnest air.

_____

## SHARON OLDS

## Missing Miss Brooks

What did you think of all those nosegays? If you were to Return
I would give you more, for all you have given us, for
your going first. The posy might have a

peony, a freesia, a tulip—an eye snack
and nostril snack, I could not get enough of
giving you those small coronation bundles, handing them
and almost bowing, tongue-tied with
respectfully adoring, with gobbling
the sight of you, the sound, the bouquets saying, mother-
—we would not be here without your song, your eye.

―――――

## KEVIN PRUFER

Kevin Prufer's newest books are *National Anthem* (Four Way Books, 2008), *In A Beautiful Country* (Four Way Books, 2011), *Churches* (Four Way Books, 2014) and the forthcoming *How He Loved Them*.

## From the Hospital

And how it snowed, I couldn't believe
the vast sweep of it when they stuck me
with the needle, then snow—and how I
loved that swirl, my hands gone numb, loved
your retreating voice, loved, in fact, you,
who sat by my bed and held my hand, and all
night long, sang.
            And then I didn't know—believe
me—if the snow was outside or inside of me,
if that was snow at the windows, or had I
closed my eyes, so my brain was a squall. I knew
your unraveling voice, though, knew you
still sang by my hospital bed, though
weakly, your voice like thinned ribbon, faintly,
and fluttering—
            far away, where the snow and
wind seemed then to thin and, just there, I
glimpsed houselights, how they lit the snow, loved
the white weather. As I drew closer to the windows, I
saw you and pressed my face to the cold glass, loved

the sight of you, mindful, in the kitchen, singing—you
who never stopped singing, not ever. Not at all.

————

## ALBERTO RÍOS

Ríos's latest collection of poems is *A Small Story about the Sky*. A National Book
Award finalist, Ríos has taught at Arizona State University for over thirty years.
He is Arizona's inaugural poet laureate and a chancellor of the Academy of
American Poets.

### Even-Keeled and At-Eased

But the truth is, I am Thursday on a Monday. I
Am the walking calendar alive of mixed-up days and dim hours. I have

A week inside of me, a week or a year, time out of order. I have contracted
With the world to behave, to try, hard, to be Monday on a Monday. I

Look like I am happiness, don't you think? On Monday, to you I have
The right laugh, and seem always to be even-keeled and at-eased.

————

## JOSHUA MARIE WILKINSON

Joshua Marie Wilkinson is the author of nine books of poetry including *Meadow
Slasher* and *Shimoda's Tavern*, both out from Black Ocean. He lives in Tucson,
Arizona, where he teaches at the University of Arizona and runs Letter Machine
Editions.

### My Own Dead

My own dead are up for visiting tonight or
they'd dreamt through the keyhole to scuttle
back into who I thought to want, & so, getting off
at the wrong stop, watery-eyed, these ghosts
are still as a whipping wind that
pauses just a moment before it says, come.

## RICHARD ZABRANSKY

Richard Zabransky lives in the Chicago area and is a professor in the writing department at Benedictine University.

### The Single Neighbor Threatens My Family

Dangerous, for I
Have ignored them. Have
You ever heard
The neighbor's dogs in
Heat, their plea rising, the
All night voices
Revealing the source of
Desire? Not human, the
Need persistent as wind,
Yet not animal, the
Groan of virulent voices.
Dangerous, the disease of
Want. They are not my
Responsibility, but a dim
Ancestry to be killed
For the sake of the children.

# My Dreams, My Works, Must Wait till after Hell

## AMA CODJOE

Ama Codjoe has roots in Memphis, Tennessee, and Accra, Ghana. She has received fellowships from Cave Canem Foundation and Callaloo. Her poems have appeared in *Tidal Basin Review, pluck!, Washington Square*, and *Callaloo* among others. She received the Rona Jaffe Graduate Fellowship from New York University, where she is currently pursuing an MFA in poetry.

### Body of a Woman, Tail of a Fish

The ocean is not something to tread on,
though there are miracles: boats with such
wooden maidens as to make legs
seem as redundant and useless as
an angel with wings. There are
other ways to move besides left
and right, up and down. For me,
the sea is something to be in,
to move through in such
times as these when the heart
sinks like a stony fish—as
deep as an anchor. With effort, I
can make the rest of me rise like smoke. I can
turn the stone's percussion into airy song. I manage
to lift myself high enough to remember
how slick the water feels as I leave it. To-
day I come a bit closer. I inhale. You go
to the Captain's log, report a sighting. I go back home.

## BILLY COLLINS

Billy Collins's latest collection is *Aimless Love: New and Selected Poems* (Random House, 2013). He is the editor of *Poetry 180: A Turning Back to Poetry* and *180 More: Extraordinary Poems for Everyday Life.*

I remember those long nights when I
would have and hold
her in our big bed with my
record player playing that song "Honey,
Honey don't you ever say bye-bye and
head on out the door" but now I
just get sent the mile and a half to the store
to pick up some things for my
wife—no more honey, just baby-wipes, butter and bread.

## ANDREA HOLLANDER

Andrea Hollander's fourth poetry collection was a finalist for the Oregon Book Award. Other honors include the Nicholas Roerich Poetry Prize, two Pushcart Prizes, and two fellowships from the National Endowment for the Arts. Writer-in-residence at Lyon College for twenty-two years, she now lives and teaches workshops in Portland, Oregon.

### Her Mouth, His Eyes

They don't undress but lie down. Her mouth close, "My dear," he says, his eyes wide. Each temptation he dreams without her has never taken place when she is here. "My love," he says, her eyes closed, his lips near. What works with other women has never worked with her. If he must change the way he speaks or moves, or if he has to wait again tonight and hope again that she'll agree to stay till dawn, he'll wait. But moonlight offers lies again, and after she says no, the heaven he anticipates will feel like hell.

## PATRICIA SPEARS JONES

Patricia Spears Jones is a Brooklyn-based African American poet/cultural activist and author of *A Lucent Fire: New and Selected Poems* from White Pine Press. She is contributing editor to *BOMB Magazine* and a senior fellow at Black Earth Institute. Recipient of National Endowment for the Arts and New York Foundation for the Arts grants, she teaches for City University of New York.

### After Hell

You can trace many bitter words, my
words and yours. Who knows how our dreams
will turn out. Will they turn out? My
days like snakes are slow moving cold. Works
in the docket, love in my pocket. I must
situate my situation. Now, I have to wait
for shimmer to shake me down. Yes, till
the very tears I fought for dry up and after
them, all is heaven after so much hell.

## JOYELLE MCSWEENEY

Joyelle McSweeney is the author of eight books of poetry, prose, drama, and essays, most recently the play *Dead Youth, or, the Leaks* and the critical book *The Necropastoral: Poetry, Media, Occults.* She edits the international press Action Books, teaches at the University of Notre Dame, and lives in South Bend, Indiana.

### ASEA

Sick, slick with reuptake inhibitor, particulated plastic, food dye, Glock my
runoff turfs a bird's gut, gives off steam. Garbage patch, cord of dreams,

supply-side, spinal column, reef-body where a gene un-my-
elin sheathes the neuron and knocks the biome up or down. How 'next' works

's a matter for a dead cat in a bottle to muddle through or out of, must-
y greenblack furze, nightvisiongoggles, gown. Stuck stuff, clot matter, wait-

ingroom seats, ab-naturally green. They suck a thigh, retreat. A wild till,
a flimsy blooming, the rest is thrip, a doomed alele. A gold god lifts his shovel. After

the storm, SONAR shudders. The shoreline wears its hairline fracture down to Hell.

---

## WILLIE PERDOMO

Willie Perdomo is the author of *The Essential Hits of Shorty Bon Bon, Smoking Lovely,* and *Where a Nickel Costs a Dime.* He has been a finalist for the National Book Critics Circle Award and Poetry Society of America Norma Farber First Book Award; winner of the International Latino Book Award in Poetry, and PEN Beyond Margins Award.

### The Best Thing to Do

It's better, you sang, to not let this love drag.
A song whose words you have written inside out.

Been the same blue in the sky since I could count to
Ten & since then I learned to release lovers to their

Fire, unguided; to get there first is to get there last.
I admit it now, there's only one way to the dregs—

When you speak to me of hearts, speak of heat &
If you get my full attention, breathe then resume.

---

## RICHARD POWERS

Richard Powers is the author of eleven novels.

### So I Wait

A dog at two a.m. starts howling No,
back yard lupine backsliding that the man
upstairs, asleep, and drugged in Dreamland can

fit nicely to his nightmare. Subtle give
and take, ancient enemies turned friends. Me:
I'm up anyway. At this hour, any
sound in this misled neighborhood is word
that wilderness will undo us all. But
morning pretends otherwise. So I wait.

---

## BOB SHACOCHIS

Bob Shacochis is a novelist, essayist, journalist, and educator. His most recent
novel, *The Woman Who Lost Her Soul*, received the Dayton Literary Peace Prize
for Fiction and was a finalist for the Pulitzer Prize for Fiction in 2014.

### Send Me Home

I was young and loved my country and I
believed in the difference I would make and bid
my home farewell and volunteered to be
what I could be, a man who kills for love, firm
in my duty, my honor, my love, till
the day arrived when they sent me home and I
wiped off the blood and took to the sky to return
to return to you, my love, to return home from
a long dream of home only to finally find Hell.

---

## AL YOUNG

Widely translated, Al Young's many books include poetry, fiction, essays,
anthologies, and musical memoirs. From 2005 through 2008 he served as
California's poet laureate. Other honors include National Endowment for the
Arts, Fulbright, and Guggenheim Fellowships; the Richard Wright Award for
Literary Excellence; and, most recently, the 2011 Thomas Wolfe Award. Visit
AlYoung.org

## Key to the Dollar Store

Just tell me who the hell am I?
What powers did I, do I hold?
What right have I to say 'my'
or 'mine' or 'me'—all honey-
glazed, all bullet-proofed and
worshipful of any gangster 'I'?

The key to the Dollar Store
hangs on my belt. Yes, 'my'
again. And what of roof, of bread,
of loving laughter? What's in?
My vinyl favorite Booker Little,
vintage, soothes me. He jars
our ears with trumpet joy and
stuff freed folks stash in cabinets.

Never one to make too much of
why we love and what, I love my
powers. I might put you in my will.

# My Own Sweet Good

## RITA DOVE

Rita Dove is a former US poet laureate (1993–1995) and recipient of the 1987 Pulitzer Prize in poetry for *Thomas and Beulah*. Her most recent poetry collections are *Sonata Mulattica* (2009) and *American Smooth* (2004). She is sole editor of *The Penguin Anthology of Twentieth-Century American Poetry* (2011). She is Commonwealth Professor of English at the University of Virginia.

## From the Sidelines

It seems I have always sat here watching men like you—
who turn heads, whose gaze is always either a kiss
or a slap or the whiplash of pure disregard. Why fret? All
you're doing is walking. You're this year's It, the
one righteous integer of cool cruising down a great-lipped
channel of hushed adoration, women turned girls
again, brightening in spite of themselves. That
brave, wilting smile—you don't see it, do you?
How she tells herself to move on; blinks until she can.

# The Near-Johannesburg Boy

## JACKIE WILLS

Jackie Wills has published five collections of poetry. The most recent is *Woman's Head as Jug* (Arc, 2013). She is a freelance writer based in Brighton, United Kingdom.

## Johannesburg 2013

Approaching the turn-off for Gold Reef City, is a
bridge where your grandmother had her pitch. Black
hair wrapped in a Venda woman's pink cloth, you still a boy,
she sold sweetcorn grilled over charcoal. We're so near,
its yellow country smell rewinds four decades. Your Johannesburg
is the routes you ran to Soweto, chased from Rocky Street hot
with cops. Later, as a choir sings on waste ground in
Hillbrow, a mechanic stares and shouts, "stay on the
road." No-one walks here—we're black, white, mixed. Hot,
dusty, we're exhausted by apartheid. Still. Beating. Time.

# Negro Hero

## JOHN KOETHE

John Koethe received the Lenore Marshall Prize for *Ninety-Fifth Street* (2010), the Kingsley Tufts Award for *Falling Water* (1997), the Frank O'Hara Award for *Domes* (1973). His most recent book is *The Swimmer* (Farrar, Straus and Giroux, 2016). He is distinguished professor of philosophy emeritus at the University of Wisconsin–Milwaukee.

### The Killer inside Me

Sometimes I wonder what I really am:
a man, a voice, an anonymous I,
or something else? I just want to be clean,
as if that might be finally enough
to get me through whatever I've got to
do to remain alive—even to kill,
if it takes that. What's thinking for,
anyway, if just to listen to them
is to follow them, to be made to do
whatever they tell me to? Who are they
in the end but myself? For though I wish
others would tell me what to do, it's me
who has to do whatever that comes to
once they've told me. Do they wish me to kill?

––––––––––

## DAVID LEHMAN

David Lehman is a poet, writer, editor, and teacher. His most recent books include the nonfiction *Sinatra's Century: One Hundred Notes on the Man and His World* (HarperCollins, 2015) and *New and Selected Poems* (Scribner, 2013). He is the editor of *The Oxford Book of American Poetry*.

## Exact Change

Let us stay here, you and I.
True, nervous—very, very nervous I had
been and am, but it remained possible to
know the change and feel it. It gave me a kick
to eat their food, drink their wine, love their
women, pray to their god, obey their law,
and that is what I did. Into
my ears their
words entered and set my teeth
on edge, and in
the ensuing parade of vices, no order
went unheeded, with progress unimpeded, but to
no end if not to save
me, you, him, her, us, and even them.

# Of De Witt Williams on His Way to Lincoln Cemetery

## WESLEY ROTHMAN

Wesley Rothman's poems have appeared in *Crab Orchard Review, Harvard Review, Mississippi Review, New England Review, Prairie Schooner,* and the anthology *Poets on Growth,* among other venues. An associate editor for *Tupelo Quarterly* and member of the board for *Salamander,* he teaches writing and cultural literatures widely.

### Incarceration Blues

Onto bulging shoulders, hammers swing
back. All hammers mean to drive low

stakes and nails and firing pins, swing
forward and back, forward and low,

farther into the ground, into deep sweet
clay. Hammers in tool belt loops on sweet

father's day cards. Each hammer a chariot
racing furiously forward. Nothing, nothing

but sleeping hammers in sidearm holsters, but
pickaxes hammering in tandem the stone of a

quarry or roadside rockslide. The jury's plain
quorum hammered into verdict, inked black

metaphors dressing a hammered-down boy.

# Of Robert Frost

## JON DAVIS

Jon Davis is the author of ten collections of poetry and translation, including *Preliminary Report* from Copper Canyon Press. He is director of the low-residency MFA program at the Institute of American Indian Arts in Santa Fe, New Mexico.

## Of Gwendolyn Brooks

There
are photos of her smiling; more common is
the downturned mouth, her hand a
puzzlement in the general din. Little
songs scrawled themselves, like lightning
in the air around her head. In
my favorite shot, her eyes look straight through his,
who must have asked the witless question. Her downcast eyes
carry sadness, pity for the unenlightened world. The iron
in that look could clang the bars at
Attica or make her lame inquisitor tremble the
interrogation. It could be she never opened her mouth
that night, could be a look was all she thought it worth. His
thoughts, if there was a *he*, are lost. Her brows
are raised, her lowered glasses ride
her nose, her skin is soft and dark. Neither
the spotlight nor the darkness can own her. Too
steady that gaze, looking past even the far
reaches of this *living*. We're compelled to look up
locked in that now eternal stare. Nor
can we know what churned beneath that cap or down
beneath the jacket, though we hope that nameless *he*
was compelled to drag it clanging through the streets. All we know is
this: when wrongs were rung in language by this poet, she was splendid.

## ISHION HUTCHINSON

Ishion Hutchinson was born in Port Antonio, Jamaica. He is an assistant professor of English at Cornell University.

### Homage: Gwendolyn Brooks

Your voice rustled the pines, handsome
as Caruso's, whose illness was glowing
amid shades where the rose ice blazed in
the hedgerow children rove with the
lightning skittles of your song, made common
in their voices with much matter and blood.

## ELIZABETH MACKLIN

Elizabeth Macklin is the author of *A Woman Kneeling in the Big City* and *You've Just Been Told*. Most recently, she has translated the Basque writer Kirmen Uribe's *Meanwhile Take My Hand*, a finalist for the 2008 PEN Award for Poetry in Translation, and Uribe's novel *Bilbao-New York-Bilbao*.

### Some Glowing in the Common Blood

I don't have much, but I have some
pomegranate kernels in a palm, glowing.
As if—They're not much, but they're in
the palm. Or now they're not. And the-
y were good. The outcome common:
common prayer for more, taut as blood.


We don't have enough. Just some
kernels in the field, durum gold, glowing
like a son of a gun out there in
the Western light. Red kernels on the
receiving end, the end most common
in the conquest; liquor in the blood.

And again I've got a handful of seeds, some
clear red kernels. When I bought them, glowing
in their market container, I didn't believe I was in
any underworld at all. They are good. The
step from the glass flowers onto the Common—
they're tart; they do not taste of blood . . .

Yet again I've got a handful of seeds, some
feast to be eaten. Each one starts out glowing,
then disappears—enough enough in
even your underworld. Is the,
would be the thought. One was once common
dosage, with something as red as blood.

------

## MICHAEL RYAN

Michael Ryan directs the MFA program in poetry at the University of California,
Irvine. *This Morning* was published in 2012 by Houghton Mifflin Harcourt,
which also published his *New and Selected Poems* in 2004. His work has won the
Kingsley Tufts Award, the Lenore Marshall Prize, and many other awards.

**No tears in the writer, no tears in the reader.**

Our iron
hearts shatter at
the
music from your mouth.

# Old Mary

## TARA BETTS

Tara Betts is the author of *Arc and Hue* and the chapbooks *7 x 7: kwansabas* and *The Greatest!: An Homage to Muhammad Ali*. Her poems have appeared in *Poetry, Gathering Ground, Bum Rush the Page, Villanelles,* both *Spoken Word Revolution* anthologies, *The Break Beat Poets,* and *Octavia's Brood.*

### Go

If you examine the embers of my
life, they will be burned to the last.
If anything is worth loving, defense
rings its resonant siren. Weaponry is
an option that boldly blacksmiths the
tender, blooming sprout of the present.

I seek methods to fortify a steely tense
because the heart requires smelting. It
wavers in the hungry yellow tongues, little
strong licks of heat that echo so many hurts.

I cannot deny what rocked and kept me,
what once made me feel safe, gone now
—ashes, dust, burned, singed, blown to
a language that wind and soil must know.

This wild whisper runs inside me, and I
must answer it or the rustling of skin shall
molt away what is left. I will never, I will not
allow myself to live half a life, so I must go.

# One Wants a Teller in a Time like This

## BOB HOLMAN

Bob Holman put together the Gwendolyn Brooks/Ntozake Shange reading at St.
Mark's Poetry Project in 1980, where Zake, during an extraordinarily vital and
musical performance, referred to Ms. Brooks's work as "poem poems." Gwen
retorted: "Here come my 'poem poems'" and launched into a reading that set fire
to the heavens.

### One Wants a Teller in a Time like This

I remember Gwen, she was one
tough cookie, her own improbable. Wants
nothing, present by disappearing, a
memory of melody. She was the Teller,
surely—snap answering Zake in
a reading at St. Mark's Church, a
teacher with a ruler. It was Time
that she was doling out, like
molecules, centuries—a time like this.

# A Penitent Considers Another Coming of Mary

## AMANDA AUCHTER

Amanda Auchter is the author of *The Wishing Tomb*, which won the 2013 PEN Center USA Award for Poetry, and *The Glass Crib*, which was awarded the 2011 Zone 3 Press First Book Award. She lives in Houston, Texas, where she teaches creative writing and literature at Lone Star College.

## Mary

The night was not blue. She asked if
there was a room. Mary
knew the answer. The stars came
dully, then bright over the field. Would
this bring cold, bring fire, bring Mary
the tender foot, the immaculate heart? Forgive
me O God. The night was not as
beautiful. A stable. Three sheep. Mothers
held their children in the street, may
have looked past Mary and
saw nothing. Not the sad
mule, the men who fell to their knees and
wept under the gold-struck star. A second,
a third hard breath. The Saviour
pressed against her spine. The furnish
of hay, sacks of spices. And us,
the later children. And what of Mary today?

The Virgin of the Cedars, Lady of the Rocks? She
the Virgin in the burnt toast, would
she cast her face into wood grain, would she not
touch the rocks, the fists of children, shake
into miracles? Dear God, I want to believe in her
quiet breath, the night filled with myrrh. To head

for shoreline, each grotto, and
lean into the improbable vision. What does she leave
for this crowd of crutches and statues, this
mouth that cannot hold prayer? This military
of wounded bodies whispering to the air,
the plastic rosaries? What does she leave but
the story unchanged? To ratify
the frankincense, the weeping fields? A
woman kisses the stones, the water. A modern
penitent, I want to gather the stable hay
in my hands, to watch the woman rise up and
be healed, to put
down her griefs, her crutches. Her
body rendered in the thrall of believing. The baby
that opened its mouth in the dark. The silence there.

                         Mary
of the Night That Was Not Blue, who would
watch her child breathe, the child not
hewn from air, but body, not to punish
but to free. The men—
their boxes of gold. The animals. The straw. If
I sing this song to myself, if Mary
is the Virgin Who Unties Knots, the story came
from the desert, a doorway, a sliver of light, tell it to me again.

# Primer for Blacks

## DOMINIQUE CHRISTINA

Dominique is a mother, and an agitator. She is a National Poetry Slam Champion, two-time winner of the Women of the World Poetry Championship, and author of two poetry books, *The Bones, The Breaking, The Balm* and *They Are All Me* and essays: *This Is Woman's Work* (SoundsTrue Publishing).

### The Hunger

By midnight a man knows where to begin
with himself, winds the clock of masculinity with
hungry fingers, slick and gaunt
from a want too thick to name and
slips roughshod down and down into himself, marvelous
in bone and birthright seeking no concession
for the wild he must become . . . and YOU

You, with dainty un-muddied midnights are
too whimsical an idea, too elaborately clean, our
faithful marches to simple jobs, the costume
of fools unrehearsed with shadows to be real and
what is left but the insult of our
un-danced fists? What is left for him but the fundamental
spending of bone?

## AARON SAMUELS

Aaron Samuels is a Cave Canem Fellow and a nationally acclaimed performer. His work has been featured on TV One's *Verses and Flow* and has appeared in many journals, including *Tidal Basin Review* and *Muzzle Magazine*. His debut collection, *Yarmulkes and Fitted Caps*, was released by Write Bloody Publishing in 2013.

## When Grandma Goes to the Moon

Grandma says that if you go to the moon, you
have to remember to come back or else you are
likely to live in a world where nobody believes our
words. Her mother wore her skin like a costume
as she secretly learned her letters by candlelight and
she would never believe that the beautiful things our
family has lived in spite of—our black—so fundamental
that even on the moon, we can peel it from our bone.
——

Grandma says if they sell tickets while she is alive, you
have to be the first in line, because when you are
on the moon, there is no such thing as compromise. Our
body floats and peels away from us—a costume
slipping away from our world like sand.
Grandma said if she goes, I have to promise our
family that I believe her, despite all I hold to be fundamental
because when she goes, we will feel it in our bones.

# Pygmies Are Pygmies Still, Though Percht on Alps

## AMY GERSTLER

Amy Gerstler's most recent book of poems is *Scattered at Sea* (Penguin, 2015). Her previous books include *Dearest Creature*, *Ghost Girl*, and *Medicine*. She teaches at the University of California at Irvine.

### Cosmic Party Crasher

Solemn philosopher, admit me to your mystic shindig! Giants
& pipsqueaks, zombies & berserkers, sheep & leaf-eared mice who
subsisted till now on crumbs and subterfuge: all bellow, bleat
and cast qualms aside to ride high tides of attunement and
interspecies ardor your hospitality incites. Scoffers may chafe,
doubting the orgies of harmony here described could be the glue in-
side us that holds cells together (and binds the universe too!) Yet their
skepticism, if they only knew (and their tears) helps it all cohere. Small
wonder, then, I beg invitations. Love replenishes itself, perennial as grass.

---

## JOHN HEGLEY

Born, London 1953, John Hegley is an English writer and performer with Anglo-French parentage. He joined Ed Berman's Interaction in London in 1978, and the company's ethos has informed his participatory style of presentation. He was poet in residence at Keats House in 2012 , plays mandolin, and draws dogs and potatoes.

### Pygmalion Director Wishes to Enliven Production

I understand those people call themselves other than Pygmies;
they may be small, but I believe their polyphonic voices could expand
this little operatic venture, which I have had a hand in.

I sense that as it stands, we tend to let our audience get cold.

But, something grander, operatically, is not impossible.

We still can make this music find its target, like a blow dart through the distant
   forest air.

# Queen of the Blues

## KIM ADDONIZIO

Kim Addonizio's new books are a collection of poems, *Mortal Trash* (W. W. Norton), and a memoir, *Bukowski in a Sundress* (Viking/Penguin). Her story collection, *The Palace of Illusions* (Counterpoint/Soft Skull) was recently released in paperback. She is online at www.kimaddonizio.com.

### Queen of the Game

The reveal. The tell. The way you show
what you don't mean to. As for me—
I'll never let you know. I've a veil. A caul. A
heavy theater curtain. I can fool a man
across a room into thinking he's inside me. What
the blues taught me is pleasure won't abide. Some will
say it's otherwise. They'll lay down their cards for love
and go all in. They'll walk away with nothing, but not me.
I'm in it for the win. What I hide, I'll hide till
hell closes down and the river's dark eye
is done with tears. Dry and alone is how I'll die.

# Riders to the Blood-Red Wrath

## JENNIFER PERRINE

Jennifer Perrine is the author of *No Confession, No Mass*, winner of the 2014 Prairie Schooner Book Prize in Poetry; *In the Human Zoo*, recipient of the 2010 Agha Shahid Ali Poetry Prize; and *The Body Is No Machine*, winner of the 2008 Devil's Kitchen Reading Award in Poetry. www.jenniferperrine.org.

### From Iraq, A Tattoo

In protest you left, but returned from the
red wrath, your single scar the national
banner blazoned on your back, an anthem
inked with needle-teeth, one hundred vampires
per second sinking into the skin at
that secret spot where spine and blades meet, the
semaphore of peace flagging in your blood.

# Riot

## DAVID BAKER

David Baker is the author of sixteen books, most recently *Scavenger Loop* (poems, W. W. Norton, 2015) and *Show Me Your Environment: Essays on Poetry, Poets, and Poems* (University of Michigan Press, 2014). He is poetry editor of the *Kenyon Review* and teaches at Denison University in Granville, Ohio.

### Stolen Sonnet

*Burn this bitch down* he
                                    said to us because—

*hands up* one said *don't*
                                    *shoot* more said but the—

all of us walking
                                    strong poor not-*poor*—

she said *black*        *loud* we're
                                    *not detainable*        were—

our loud sanity
                                    freezing        sweaty—

riot is the language
                                    of the unheard and—

I swear he said it's
                                    *not just*        unpretty—

so it's not the law
                                    *don't bust my store* and—

*any handy angel*

        walk with us      they—

shouting pushing but

        what about him      were—

*and took a pack of*

        *cigarillos*      coming—

what did he see when

        he saw *It* now toward—

*taking aim*      running

        fast away from him—

        *

so we all *went down*

        *in the smoke and fire—*

---

## ASIA CALCAGNO

Asia Calcagno is a poet, performer, and English teacher from Chicago. Her work has been featured in *Learn Then Burn 2, Glass Mountain, Youth Voice Nation,* and *Women in REDzine.* She has been awarded the Charles B. Palmer Poetry Prize from the Academy of American Poets.

### Gravestones

Good gracious. *You again.* And it is always you
asking to borrow cigarettes and time. We are
exhaling on the curb. Mouths heating with a
debate. Yellow town lights bleed desperate
wings against our faces. Testimonies of a good man
tonight. The "Jesus Camp" story, stoicism and
smoke smiles. *My mother shot a man.* The

ember pinches your fingertips with a desperate
kiss. *Does that make her a bad woman? We all die.*
*Does it matter?* The extinguished filters are expensively
buried. We woke with our names on gravestones today.

---

## RACHEL DEWOSKIN

Rachel DeWoskin is the award-winning author of the novels *Blind* (Penguin, 2014); *Big Girl Small* (FSG, 2011); *Repeat after Me* (Overlook, 2009); and the memoir *Foreign Babes in Beijing* (Norton, 2005). Her poems have been published widely in journals including *Ploughshares*. She is on the fiction faculty at the University of Chicago.

### Taunting the Turkey Vultures with Love

We dove off cliffs, down, down while birds rose, itched
and circled, waited, lost us to life. *Ha!* You and I were made instantly
hungry, lively, driven, shot through with silver beneath
a bubbled narrative, the opposite of death, cool love and wonder among the
many fast fish who sliced by. You are how it feels to float up nourished,
laughing, even the shadows of fingered wings gone, sun whole, the sky hot white.

---

## HELEN FROST

Helen Frost is the author of two poetry collections, eight novels-in-poems, and four picture books. Her awards include a National Endowment for the Arts Poetry Fellowship, the New York Historical Society's Children's History Book Prize, and the Lee Bennett Hopkins Poetry Award. She lives in Fort Wayne, Indiana.

### Softer Sounds

Prison gates clang shut, locking in
memories of a thousand softer sounds: seas
breaking against shells crushed into sand, leaves in
treetops brushing one against another in the windsweep

of a cityscape where they
sent their breeze to cool us. Remember? We were
jumping rope, that slap against the sidewalk, when a black
bird swooped in to carry off your gum wrapper, and—
it didn't take so much back then—we all laughed out loud.

## LIZ LOCHHEAD

Liz Lochhead was born in Motherwell, Scotland, in 1947 and is the current
Makar (national poet) of Scotland. A prolific playwright as well as a poet and
performer of poetry all over the United Kingdom and beyond, she is interested
in the next generation and is a patron of many organizations who support them,
particularly in the arts and creative fields.

### Beyond It

The bad weather is trying to get in
so veils of rain become blatterings, seas
over-arch, they pound and rake our shores. In
they come—far, far beyond the high-tide mark with windsweep
and drag, splintering all they suck back in. They
make a nothing of all things that once were
our all-in-all, stood proud. The skies go black
with thick murk, this impenetrable cloud, and
more-than-weather stirs one boiling broth of chaos, irresistible and loud.

## ROGER ROBINSON

Roger Robinson is a Trinidadian writer and musician who has lived in London
for twenty years. He was chosen by *Decibel* as one of fifty writers who have
influenced the black-British writing canon, was shortlisted for the OCM Bocas
Poetry Prize, and highly commended by the Forward Poetry Prize. He has toured
internationally with the British Council and is a cofounder the international
writing collective Malika's Kitchen.

## Brixton Revo 2011

In caps, hoodies and bandannas, they went
through Brixton like locusts, mowing a field down.
Streaming from small alleys, they flooded in.
Armed with bottles and scrap metal, they smelled the
petrol in the air and the ashen taste of smoke
on their tongues. They ransacked phone shops and
darted in an out trainer shops lit by flares of fire.
As thick black smoke billowed, they stood still and
for a few minutes surveyed what they'd broken:
the crumpled iron shutters, jagged stalactites of glass.
Then like stray dogs they roamed the streets and
thought what next they could do to pump their blood.

# The Rites for Cousin Vit

## MONA ARSHI

Mona Arshi was born in London, England, into a Sikh Punjabi family. She worked as a human-rights lawyer before she became a poet. Her debut collection *Small Hands* was published by Liverpool University Press. Mona won the Forward Prize for best first collection in 2015.

### Blue Finch

Blue finch what are you? She
winds herself up and rises
like a blue finch. She surrenders in
flight (because the sky spares no thought for her), the
bird dying a little in the dreamy sunshine.
The yellow beak issues one timorous note and look there
she comes to rest on my clean hands. She prepares herself, she
calls, calls again-a secret hymn . . . she goes!

———

## HOA NGUYEN

Hoa Nguyen is the author of four full-length collections of poetry including *As Long as Trees Last* (Wave Books, 2012) and *Red Juice, Poems 1998–2008* (Wave Books, 2014). She currently lives in Toronto, Ontario, where she teaches poetics privately and at Ryerson University.

### Offbeat

*"[one] anchored in the world of humans and the other in that of the gods"*
—*Nathaniel Mackey*

The month that works the pierce of
Mouths      Aperture of lips      Pregnancy
of the self      It is soul birth to grand guitars

like the slurring cords      sliding      The limping and
the stutter     One short leg      one long      Bridgework-
dance    She dances limply to speak      Walks

---

## WILLIAM STOBB

William Stobb is the author of five poetry collections, including *Absentia* and
the National Poetry Series selection *Nervous Systems*, both from Penguin Books.
Stobb is associate dditor at *Conduit*, and chair of the Wisconsin Poet Laureate
Commission. He lives in La Crosse, Wisconsin.

### Cousin

Something. The way she'd say oh
nothing, oh dear, whatever oh

this mix got a little too
strong must've been too much

rum but then it was too
much day wasn't it much too much.

Impossible just to break even
I felt. Then and now

this function smothered in surmise
like every passage she

underlines burns a little, rises
to hand, to lend a hand up in

good standing like posture bears the
self into its moment, sunshine

in a field meaning there
could be a place for us. She

means time, love, goes.

## DAN SULLIVAN

Dan "Sully" Sullivan has a BA in poetry from Columbia College. He is a
Gwendolyn Brooks Open Mic Award recipient and founder of the Urban
Sandbox, a youth-focused poetry series in Chicago, currently in its thirteenth
year. His first book of poems, *The Blue Line Home* is available from EM-Press.

## There Are Mornings

Last night was a sommelier's upturned wrist. It resisted the slops
then tottered home and found crisp sheets to sprawl. Sleep was the
middle distance, a wince begging to become touch. This is the bad
news. Some mornings do not age well. They pour without trill in wine,
the coffee all grit, no filter. Slow yawns plod across
the floorboards, shirk into the knots. I move as if her
song still steams the mirror, flats still dresser-side, shantung
swaying from bedpost. There are mornings like this, when the stillness talks.

# Sadie and Maud

## FLORENCE LADD

Florence Ladd's poems have appeared in *Women's Review of Books, Progressive, Rockhurst Review, Sweet Auburn, Beyond Slavery,* and *Transition.* Her chapbook, *Reclaiming Rose,* was published (2015) by Finishing Line Press. She is the author of the novels *Sarah's Psalm, The Spirit of Josephine,* and *Jason Henderson's Senior Year.*

## Sadie and Maud

Sadie had a sister named Maud
applauded wherever she went
for her scholarly achievements to
the delight of kin with no college
who failed to see talents of Sadie
devoted to family and so she stayed
til their parents' end in their home.

Home, in need of repair, a handyman
stayed there often into the night with
Sadie who knew how to charm as her
college-bred sister couldn't do
to this day; the neighbors, alarmed,
went to the pastor to inform him of
Maud's sister's wayward ways,

Maud, told to scold Sadie, instead
went to the handyman asking him
to declare his intent (in terms she'd learned in
college); he confessed he planned to marry
Sadie, but decided to wait 'til his business
stayed steady and he could build a dream
home for a happy ending for himself and his lady.

# GAIL CARSON LEVINE

Gail Carson Levine's poems have appeared in *Louisville Review, Sugar House Review*, and the anthologies *Bigger than They Appear, On the Dark Path*, and *The Cancer Poetry Project 2*. Her books for children include *Ella Enchanted* and the poetry collection *Forgive Me, I Meant to Do It*.

## Maud and Sadie

Sadie's childhood friend, tall, pigeon-toed Maud,
had an umbrella hat and a gray parrot who went
*Well done, dopey dingo!* and, *What are you up to,
tootsie?* Maud took the parrot along to college.
Her lame, bloodshot beagle she gave to Sadie,
who got a job as a vet tech in town and stayed
with her mom, though she went prowling at
night to collect kittens and carry them home.

Maud moved to Maui minus the parrot. Sadie
groomed poodles on the side and scraped
up cash to rescue the bird. Her theory of a life
evolved to this: Do without the Mauds; stick with
fur, four feet, feathers, talons. But years later a
better Maud returned, paid the friendship fine
with "Sorry!" then asked, "Nature red in tooth
and paw?" Sadie smiled. "Yes. I'll clip. You comb."

# The Second Sermon on the Warpland

## DANIELLE CADENA DEULEN

Danielle Cadena Deulen is the author of two poetry collections, *Our Emotions Get Carried Away beyond Us* (winner, Barrow Street Book Contest) and *Lovely Asunder* (winner, Miller Williams Poetry Prize) and a memoir, *The Riots* (winner, AWP Prize, creative nonfiction).

### Medics

Let us stitch the wounds shut, rub salve
into the skin, salvage

the torn limbs, the sinew-song in
the tender throat. Let us mend the

punctured lung, the vertigo spin
of the inner ear, endorse

our names on the slips that admit the
writhing. There is splendor

in the scalpel's glint, the splashes
of red in the heart. Let us stylize

the nerves, the vascular canvas, the
split in the brain, so beautifully flawed.

Let us unbury the bullet, know the utility
of sunrise, the flag drawn up like a prop

over pitched tents, each like an "A"—
the last sound in every mouth. Let us malign

the malignant, cut out the ill, or
make it bright. Let us work in the failing

darkness. Let us suture each other with light.

———————

## MARK DOTY

Mark Doty is the author of nine books of poems, most recently *Deep Lane* (Norton, 2015) and *Fire to Fire: New and Selected Poems*, which won the National Book Award for Poetry in 2008. He teaches at Rutgers University and lives in New York City.

### Advice from Ms. Brooks, With Elaborations

Conduct
your
blooming
—it's the little words—in,
of, a, the—
that hold the noise
and firefall of the larger world together, and
keep things each to each with the thinnest whip
of
speech and sense—what we do when we stand facing into the
Whirlwind.

Suppose you could learn to conduct
the days, your
hours blooming
then fading in
the hush after, the
beautiful rising and falling of noise,
that silence that signals and
launches the world again with the whip-
crack of
the
new, before it goes tumbling in the whirlwind.

Conduct
the hours of your
orchestra, blooming
then fading in
the hush after, the
not-noise
that signals and
new-launches the world with the whip
crack of
music, the lashing start and stop and begin: the
lived sound of the whirlwind.

––––––––

## CHERISE A. POLLARD

Cherise A. Pollard, PhD, is a professor of English at West Chester University of Pennsylvania. A Cave Canem Fellow, her work has appeared or is forthcoming in several journals including *Rattle*, *Pittsburgh Poetry Review*, *Connotations Press*, *Healing Muse*, *Affilia*, *African American Review*, and *5AM*.

### Reflections on Invictus

Oppression, racism's root, must conduct
itself like a disease, right? Your
lesions are rising, sometimes blooming
where they cannot be seen. In
pink places, interstitial spaces, the
flesh opens, releasing the body's noise.
What more can be said about suffering so pure, and
yet so deeply and humanely black that the whip
of understanding snags our backs? Of
course, there is something familiar in the
desire to control what you cannot see: racism's whirlwind.

## MAUREEN SEATON

Maureen Seaton has authored seventeen poetry collections, both solo and collaborative—most recently, *Fibonacci Batman: New and Selected Poems* (Carnegie Mellon University Press, 2013) and *Caprice: Collected, Uncollected, and New Collaborations* (with Denise Duhamel, Sibling Rivalry Press, 2015). She teaches poetry at the University of Miami, Florida.

### Bigly in the Wild Weed

*For LMA, for twenty-six years*

We're so in love lover you're the one whose
holy self tilts a rose-wise wish-hot half-black
planet on its punk-chin alarm side with hands
I could build an entire house with or assemble
a peace to write songs for or let's suck oranges
now before Florida floods and we're at sea. Is
it true we do exist without our former tom-tom
selves our ponderous hearts our swell hearted
old ghosts? I can't unimagine our croon it goes
zinging through love-beguiled blood our love in
the time of astonishment. What are we bearing
toward if not nothing recognizable our oranges
sap-bloody and sweet as all our only fruits and
everything bubble-upping bright sugar boom?

# The Sermon on the Warpland

## MALIKA BOOKER

Malika Booker is a British writer of Guyanese and Grenadian parentage. *Breadfruit* was published by Flipped Eye in 2008, and *Pepper Seed* was published by Peepal Tree Press in 2013. She was the inaugural poet in residence at the Royal Shakespeare Company, a Cave Canem Fellow, and Cultural Fellow in Creative Writing at Leeds University.

### A Parable of Sorts

We danced to rancorous tunes on spiked ground and
our knees sang with each puncture, so that several

agouti colonies, melanic in our russet strengths,
learned as wild rats to scurry or guard ourselves from

skin-spite. Immune from nocturnal drowsiness
we strong belly creatures assembled, campaigned;

gyrated to blowed trumpets and cradled songs, but,
us black rats with our rogue swagger that spoke

of foreign ports, pranced our survival shuffle in
night's murky dance halls. Each step our single

prayer, each jab, our benediction. This tart sermon
containered our septic hurts and lean swaggers. On

the strike of dawn, we skittered from shadows, the
redeemed walking day's straight-road into warp land.

# A Song in the Front Yard

## JOHN BURNSIDE

John Burnside is a multi-prize-winning poet, fiction writer, and memoirist. He teaches at the University of St. Andrews.

### A Peek at the Back

They are out in the dark, but no one can ever say where:
black-stockinged women who know when it's
time to get rough;
lovers who pledge false troth in abandoned cars and
lie down under the stars in untended
gardens; frost-seasoned girls and
boys who will always be hungry
for touch and forgiveness, half-crazy from years of weed
and homebrewed jack. Wherever the moonflower grows

through chain-link, cream-white and pink, there's a
summer that never ends, like the sense of a girl
at the back of my head, in that story where somebody gets
the one thing he always wanted, then gives it away, already half-sick
of possession, that unwitting choice of
having or being had, and no chance in this world of a
life that remains to be told, like a death, or a rose.

---

## PETER COOLEY

Peter Cooley has published nine books of poetry, the most recent of which is *Night Bus to the Afterlife* (Carnegie Mellon, 2014). He is director of creative writing and Senior Mellon Professor of the Humanities at Tulane University in New Orleans and has just been made Louisiana poetry laureate.

## My Life Has Been No Smaller Than My Mind

encircling the four corners of a room I've
I've kept inside me since my childhood. stayed
Every wall has a window to watch me in
while I assemble landscape on landscape—the
peaks, gorges, sierras, icebergs, flatlands, front
each heft and texture hewn into a song. yard
I have such little imagination all
the world must begin every time again, my
every flower's red seen for the first instant, life


and then that garden, once more—paradise.

---

## MARIAHADESSA EKERE TALLIE

Mariahadessa Ekere Tallie is the author of *Dear Continuum: Letters to a Poet Crafting Liberation* (Grand Concourse Press) and *Karma's Footsteps* (Flipped Eye). She is the poetry editor of the literary magazine *African Voices*. Tallie's work is the subject of the short film, *I Leave My Colors Everywhere.*

## Gap-Toothed Woman

They brace themselves. I wear
my gap-toothed smile, the
mouth of beauty. Journeys of brave
women, salty & blue. Fula hands mending stockings,
nursing strangers, stitching lives. Bleeding women of
cane & cotton, forced women dreading night,
blues women, salty & bleeding, surviving & black.

These teeth an inheritance more inviting than lace
the driver says and
he knows I am his stolen sister, strut
of my eyes, spaced stars in the sky of my mouth travel back and down
strands of tangled heritage, the
me before these shores, these streets.

They brace themselves, teeth and words aligned with
what shipped them here. They paint
smiles and deference on
across their lips. My
gap-toothed rebellion is an altar. My ancestors gather in the hills of my face.

---

## AISLING FAHEY

Aisling Fahey has performed in locations across England, America, and Ireland,
including the Houses of Parliament and Glastonbury. She is a member of the
Burn after Reading collective and Barbican Young Poets and was young poet
laureate for London 2014–15. She has appeared on BBC Radio 4, BBC
London, and ITV London Tonight.

### Walthamstow Central

End of the Victoria Line. Last stop. Where
the stragglers jolt awake, realising it's
the last train of the night. Hands rough,
clasping an Evening Standard and
a hip flask. Their bodies are untended
mazes, faulty circuit boards. And
we watch them spark. Their eyes are hungry.
The boys on my road smell of leaving and weed.
It is not the flowers, but the boys and the night that grows.

---

## LINDSAY HUNTER

Lindsay Hunter is a writer living in Chicago. She is the author of the novel *Ugly
Girls* and the story collections *Don't Kiss Me* and *Daddy's*.

### Our Home

You see how I make the bed, how I've
put away the dishes, stayed
home with you most nights, stayed in

with our things, turning off lights, checking the
locks, unlocking so I can lock the front
door, never looking into the yard
where I might see me, fourteen years old, looking in, all
heart, a nice way of putting it, all genitals, a better way of putting it, my
dear, I've throbbed so long this body's more beat than life.

————————

## ANGELA JOHNSON

Angela Johnson was born in Alabama in 1961 and is an award-winning
American children's book and poetry author with over forty books. She has
won three Coretta Scott King Awards and the Michael Printz Award. In
recognition of her of body of work she was named a MacArthur Fellow.

### Troubled

The last time I saw her she had a bucket hat on
trippin' down the avenue on account
her mama had heard of
all the troubled things she did last
fall and into the winter.
The food truck man said he
saw her just before he sold
out quick of our
favorite burritos to kick back
with—then heard the sound of a bus pulling out the gate.

————————

## JACOB POLLEY

Jacob Polley is the author of three books of poems, most recently *The Havocs*
(Picador, 2012), which received the Geoffrey Faber Memorial Prize in 2013, and
a novel, *Talk of the Town* (Picador, 2009). Born in Cumbria, England, he teaches
at Newcastle University.

## Twelve Weeks

We call you Bean. Where
have you been? How long it's
been before you, little rough-
smooth, little he-she; and
who knew there lay untended
such a plot between us, and
a hunger, too? Who knew we were so hungry
to give ourselves over to you, sweet weed?
Your father weathers. Your mother grows.

————————

## JON SANDS

Jon Sands is the author of *The New Clean*. His work has been published widely
and anthologized in *The Best American Poetry 2014*. He is the program director
of the Dialogue Arts Project and the co-founder of Poets in Unexpected Places.
He tours extensively, but lives in Brooklyn, New York. www.jonsands.com.

## Statue

What good manners and khakis can I wear
to cover this heartsick tune: the
ache I plead will flower like a brave
knife to the hand's palm? I am stocking
myself with napalm each time the spark of
nicety flicks my bottom lip, and promises night-
time is when I will be my own company: sky, black
like my eyes. The sheath of politeness' lace
strewn across my hardwood bedroom floor, and
the window's danger beckons my vicious strut.
But I wouldn't even know where to go. Sit down.
No jaw I can wishbone, law I can break. The
unanswerable phone that does not ring. The streets,
a sweet danger that have passed me by with-
out noticing. I won't even risk falling in love. I paint
murals up to the ceiling of windows I say I'll shatter on

a different night. My body, a hushed twilight. My
wayward pyre: a slow rise beneath a stone face.

------------

## DIANE SEUSS

Diane Seuss's most recent collection, *Four-Legged Girl,* was published by
Graywolf Press in 2015. Her second book, *Wolf Lake, White Gown Blown
Open,* won the Juniper Prize for Poetry and was published by the University of
Massachusetts Press in 2010. Seuss is writer in residence at Kalamazoo College.

### back yard song

Since it's just me here I've
found the back and stayed
there most of the time, in
rain and snow and the
no moon nights, dodging the front
I used to put up like a yard
gussied and groomed, all
edged and flower-lined, my
bottled life.
Uncorked, I had a thought: I
want the want
I dreamed of wanting once, a
quarter cup of sneak-peek
at what prowls in the back, at
what sings in the
wet rag space behind the garage, back

where the rabbits nest, where
I smell something soupish, sour and dank and it's
filled with weeds like rough
cat tongues and
the wind is unfostered, untended,
now that it's just me here and
I am so hungry

for the song that grows tall like a weed
grows, and grows.

When I was a
little girl
my ma said a woman gets
tired and sick
of the front yard, of
kissing the backside of a
rose.

---

## EVIE SHOCKLEY

Evie Shockley is the author of four collections of poetry, most recently *The New Black* (Wesleyan University Press), which won the 2012 Hurston/Wright Legacy Award in Poetry. She has also published a critical study, *Renegade Poetics: Black Aesthetics and Formal Innovation in African American Poetry* (University of Iowa Press). Shockley is creative editor of *Feminist Studies* and associate professor of English at Rutgers University–New Brunswick.

### song in the back yard

*a golden shovel for rihanna*

the more you see     the less you see me     tattoos and
thighs crowd your eyes     i'm young but i've seen scenes i'd
pay well to unwitness     plays as old as power     an ancient script     you like
my hair     my ass     my tits     if you had to
sell my voice     how would you package it     would it be
pretty in pink     with dancehall in my spit and a
childhood of training in denial     mi make it good girl gone bad
gone red     seen red     seen blue black scream-swollen song scene     woman
down     i didn't do it     this was done to me     and my love is too

complicated to have thrown back in my face     and
it's got nothing to do with the clothes i wear
he was my friend     he was my father     i was my mother     the

ancient script again      now casting a new generation      you got to be brave
when every minute of your day is a press / release      my stockings
my sheerest armor      my filly signal      just one sign of
the fearless core you do not want to mess wit      my strength is night-black
is island-rock      is hard but alive as coral reef      the lace

the caribbean sea makes      no surprise *i'm so hard* eh      *chains and*
*whips excite me*      i love leather      i will strut
the red carpet in any city in the world      in necklines down
to there      shorts rising up to here      but i'm the
barbadian mirage      the weed-hungry boys in the back alleys and busy streets
of the world      dem cah look but never touch      i'm dizzy with
power      but rubber-muscled from the weight of the role i model      mi paint
mi politics pon mi lips for de young girls to read      slip on
courage like stilettos      and in return      fair-weather fans bring roses to my
door      real love brings an *umbrella*      shelter for my only human face

---

## JEANANN VERLEE

Jeanann Verlee is author of *Said the Manic to the Muse* and award-winning *Racing Hummingbirds*. She has also been awarded the Third Coast Poetry Prize and the Sandy Crimmins National Prize for Poetry. Her work has appeared in *Rattle, failbetter, Yemassee,* and *Adroit,* among others.

## Careful the Blood

Mama was a cool swathe of sad bones but
shimmied hard as a wrecking ball. I
swore I'd never move like that, never say
*ass-shake* or *hipswing*. Never hiss, *It's*
*the blues makes my tongue wet.* "She a fine
ginger," they'd say, "that arch, bend." Honest
women make dangerous property. Don't I
know what grief in a good woman can do?

Press her silk mouth to a Budweiser and
an entire pool hall would stop, lean in. I'd

be a liar to say she wasn't proud, didn't like
all those eyes reaching their long arms out to
stroke thigh, neck, each freckle. Finally to be
the spotlight, to unnerve a room. Just a
quiet country girl, legs enough to act bad.
Survive is the thing learned first. No woman
juke box without reason. Misery gotta dance, too.

This is how she mounted sorrow. Rum and
patent leather. With Bessie singing, she'd wear
floorboards down to dust. Through smoke, the
back room boys entered, all hands and brave
bearded smiles. Making prayer of stockings,
garters, the hot pearl shimmer of slick lips. Of
the bass, the thrum and thrum and night-black
wisps of sweat, flesh, and the gospel of lace.

Here I learned to move. Swore never, and
failed. It's in the blood. Mama's long strut,
hard jaw. When baby died, she counted down
the ticks of her own pulse. When papa left, the
hard in her bones hardened. Easier in the streets
when her wicked bloomed, her backhand. With
each new grief, she soured. I learned to paint
over, hide scars. Honest women last, keep on.
We make dangerous property. Careful my
hips, my bite. Careful the smile on my face.

---

## FRED WAH

Fred Wah lives in Vancouver, British Columbia. He was Canada's fifth
Parliamentary Poet Laureate. Recent collections *Is a Door, Sentenced to Light,* and
*Scree: The Collected Earlier Poems, 1962–1991* are available from Talonbooks.

Somewhere where
That clean line of ridge snow it's

A final place rough
But blue and cold and
The distances left untended
Only to return to this and
"This unchill" still hungry
For love, that weed
A memory of the future grows.

------

"This unchill" from Margaret Avison's "New Year's Poem."

# The Sonnet-Ballad

## NICK LANTZ

Nick Lantz lives in Texas and teaches in the creative-writing program at Sam Houston State University.

### Deployed

I built a room      inside you      where I could pace the floor. Oh
but now I'm just a footfall      that won't repeat.      Mother
of my children,      translate this sand.      Mother
of my regret,      please bury      my name in the yard where
the dog      can't dig it up.      At night, the base is
dark as a rifle barrel.                  And happiness?

Ask the men      who herd goats      in the shale hills. They
look at their sandals      when our convoys      roll past. I took
a stone      from a bombed village      and put it under my
bunk. At night      it sings      a lover's
song, full      of things stones love:      clouds, the tallness
of trees      before they fall.      Please      don't turn off
the porch light:                  I need it to
see in this place      where even the dog and his tail      are at war.

---

## JAMAAL MAY

Jamaal May is the award-winning author of *Hum* and *The Big Book of Exit Strategies*. His poetry explores the spaces between opposites to render a sonically rich argument for the interconnectivity of people as well as the worlds they inhabit. From Hamtramck and Detroit he co-directs OW! Arts with Tarfia Faizullah.

## The Names of Leaves In War

They took light from our eyes. So possessive.
Took the moisture from our throats. My arms,
my lips, my sternum, sucked dry, and
lovers of the kickback say, *look, there is beauty.*
Tallness only made me a long target made of
off-kilter limbs. I'd fall either way. I should get a
*to-the-death* tattoo or a metal ribbon of some sort.
War took our prayers like nothing else can,
left us dumber than remote drones. Make
me a loyal soldier and I'll make you a
lamenting so thick, metallic, so tank-tread-hard.
Now make tomorrow a gate shaped like a man.
I can't promise, when it's time, that I won't hesitate,
cannot say I won't forget to return in fall and
guess the names of all the leaves before they change.

---

## MICHELE PARKER RANDALL

Michele Parker Randall is the author of *Museum of Everyday Life* (Kelsay Books, 2015). A recent finalist for the Peter Meinke Poetry Prize, her work has appeared or is forthcoming from *Painted Bride Quarterly, Potomac Review, Newport Review* (First Prize Flash Fiction), and elsewhere. Michele teaches at Stetson University.

## Breaking House

In this settling of what's what,
there is no all-seeing—I
sense what I will or can
do, what is still of any use
to me. My home stands, an
erudite but now empty
sort of heart-cup
my heart still-beats for.

## VIRGINIA EUWER WOLFF

Virginia Euwer Wolff is a fiction writer for young readers whose novel *True Believer* won the National Book Award in 2001. She is a mother, grandmother, lapsed schoolteacher, lifetime second violinist, and Smith College graduate who has lived in rural, unelectrified Oregon and in Hell's Kitchen, Manhattan.

## Dusk

Dark sky-dash of birds in the valley, Oh
flap and flash, chorale of wings over deep water, mother,
your bird-ships sail, lift again and dive again, mother,
if you could alight in my hand, or keen around me still where
I stand and lean up this hill, could I hear how shimmer-clear your song is
and tell myself we, your lightning eye and I, have discovered happiness?

## TIMOTHY YU

Timothy Yu is the author of *100 Chinese Silences* (Les Figues) and three chapbooks: *15 Chinese Silences* (Tinfish), *Journey to the West* (Barrow Street), and, with Kristy Odelius, *Kiss the Stranger* (Corollary). He is associate professor of English and Asian American studies at the University of Wisconsin-Madison.

## Moon

That cloud-hid moon made a silent Oh
every night my daughter asked for her mother
and maybe I told her the moon was her mother
not knowing if tomorrow she'd ask me where
the moon was hiding when the sun is
shining or if the sun is happiness

# Speech to the Young, Speech to the Progress-Toward

## MARILYN NELSON

Marilyn Nelson, the recipient of the 2012 Frost Medal, is a chancellor of the Academy of American Poets and poet-in-residence of the Poets Corner at the Cathedral of St. John the Divine. Her most recently published books are *My Seneca Village* (Namelos, 2015) and *American Ace* (Dial, 2016).

### Bird-Feeder

Approaching seventy, she learns to live,
at last. She realizes she has not
accomplished half of what she struggled for,
that she surrendered too many battles
and seldom celebrated those she won.
Approaching seventy, she learns to live
without ambition: a calm lake face, not
a train bound for success and glory. For
the first time, she relaxes her hands on the
controls, leans back to watch the coming end.
Asked, she'd tell you her life is made out of
the things she didn't do, as much as the
things she did do. Did she sing a love song?
Approaching seventy, she learns to live
without wanting much more than the light in
the catbird window seat where, watching the
voracious fist-sized tweets, she hums along.

# Still Do I Keep My Look, My Identity

## MONIZA ALVI

Moniza Alvi was born in Pakistan and grew up in Hertfordshire. Three of her collections, including the most recent *At the Time of Partition* (Bloodaxe Books, 2013), have been shortlisted for T. S. Eliot Prize. She received a Cholmondeley Award in 2002.

### I still don't know

I don't know who I am. Still
don't—and then I think I do
a bit. My song: I am. I am. I am. I
give it to the sea of life to keep,

it washes it away and sends it back. My
slice, bright slice. A self. Look
I'm falling through my hands, my
arms, my glance. Identity.

---

## RAYMOND ANTROBUS

Raymond Antrobus is a British Jamaican poet and former lead educator on the Spoken Word Education MA Programme at Goldsmiths University in London. He is also cocurator of popular London poetry events Chill Pill (Soho Theatre and the Albany) and Keats House Poets.

### The Artist

There are good reasons to tweezer each
word that you give a body
to pronounce your stance on what has
carried your cells with its
language of what you might call living for art.

## HANNAH SRAJER

Hannah Srajer is a student at Princeton University studying history and creative writing. Her work has been featured in *Sierra Nevada Review, Nassau Literary Review, Venture,* and other publications. She hopes to write a book of poems someday. She is thankful to Mr. Kahn, Mr. Gilmer, Mr. Lind, and the entire Oak Park and River Forest High School spoken word community for fostering and encouraging her poetry.

### Third Infidelity

Mother locks herself in
the bathroom, sterile castle

with no moat. No latch or
lock or chain can conta(in)

her sensible grief, the shack
she builds with

out us. Squatter in rags
in her own home, or

his. Marriage is a dirty robe,
a cover for nakedness through

which I was born, a good
girl with nothing

but what was built f(or)
me, the stones

# Strong Men, Riding Horses

## ONI BUCHANAN

Oni Buchanan is the author of three poetry books: *Must a Violence* (Kuhl House Poets, 2012), *Spring* (University of Illinois Press, 2008), and *What Animal* (University of Georgia Press, 2003). Buchanan is the founder and director of the Ariel Artists management company, representing classical musicians pursuing visionary performance projects.

### Pasted to Stars Already

Essential lack of the presence of women. Except
for the occasional brothel lass, that
bawdy-humored, lace-gartered heroine. Strong
for her bevy of plaster-powdered ladies. Masked. Men

as dull yet dangerous ducklings whose quackings are
divvied up among capable mothers. Lead these desert-
desiccated doggies to water's edge. Be eyed.
Be sighed. It's all a grander compromise. Except

for the quality of crinolines. Except that
scars in daylight can be creamed away. Strong
perfumes to placate daring odors. Wrangler Men
just love the lumping in. The house-bound husbands are

tethered to a different punchline, their loyalty pasted
to detergent brands. Outlaw or outright imposter to
an idealized and vital self, the Near-Miss Life stars
You in pre-fabricated roles, the outcome known already.

## TISHANI DOSHI

Tishani Doshi is an award-winning poet, novelist, and dancer. She has published six books of fiction and poetry, and her work has been translated into several languages. She has worked as a dancer with the Chandralekha troupe since 2001. She lives in Tamil Nadu, India. www.tishanidoshi.com

### Strong Men, Riding Horses

The men in my life come back strong.
Fat off the agony of summers gone these men
no longer think to write or call before riding
into dreams with Lugers and Stetsons. On horses.
All wrong. They charge in. They charge in
like assassins through floorboards and fairings. The
men in my life grow spring-like out West.
Cowboys with staches and gingham chests, adrift on
the lawns of banishment. O, the infinity of a
grown man who waits. Days unbutton as a range
of mountains emerging from under cloud. Five
years unravel into five hundred. Five hundred
into hunger. So many disappeared miles.
The men in my life hold secrets like eggs. A
thousand
would-be husbands circle the border, reaching
for navel, face, breastplate, rope. And from
everything you imagined that was not, comes dawn,
spidery and wet, releasing them back to
the West, to where they rode in from. Sunset
restores them with harmonicas, rested
and keen for a-battering again. Yesterday's blue-
tongued blades of grass. All the paths to
longing are recurring and paved with orange
trees, earthquakes, other women's men. From
here the future blooms like a prehistoric fish of hope:
flat-headed, obdurate. The lesson being to
submerge, to listen to the music of bones crying

as they are changed from gills to hoof. Except
for the fossils gathered at our feet, that
insist with an architecture ancient and strong,
what can we say about empires of harmony, of men
who ride horses? Treacherous as they are,
we must counter these phantoms, desert-eyed.
Except
for sleep, nothing is ever finished, and all that
remains of night is a rooftop in summer, a strong
wind from the sea, birds, hay, a family of men
with high foreheads, picking their teeth. They are
lurching toward you with roses and pasted-
down hair. Breath jangly with fear. To
have survived the ever-present restlessness of stars.
Wake now. All that we mourn is here already.

———————

## DOUGLAS KEARNEY

Douglas Kearney's *Patter* (Red Hen Press, 2014) was a finalist for the California Book Award in Poetry. *The Black Automaton* (Fence Books, 2009) was a National Poetry Series selection. His libretti include a western, *Dead Horses*. He lives with his family in the Santa Clarita Valley. He teaches at CalArts.

## The Strong Strong Men Riding Strong Strong Horses after the West

[reel 1]


in The West, men strong
men, the riding men riding horses men.
west men! west! the men riding
The West. the horses
strong. horses in the men in
The West riding the
horses. strong, the men in The West.

[reel 2]

a hundred miles. a range. on
a range reaching five hundred,
a thousand miles. a range
reaching miles and miles, five
thousand miles. a hundred
thousand miles and miles.
a thousand strong men reaching The West. a
thousand strong men riding a thousand
strong horses. The West: a reaching.

[reel 3]

the sun rested, orange, from
dawn to sunset in The West. dawn
sun riding the strong men riding the horses to
The West. too, the strong men rested, sunset
on the orange range. the strong rested
men set to reaching the sunset. blue,
The West, from the too strong men. to
arrange The West, the men wrested the sun from in the orange

[reel 4]

to the blue. the strong men from The West from
the horses from the range! hope
on reaching the orange west to
wrest the sun to the blue. The West crying
a thousand blue miles of riding/reaching blue except
the orange riding that
blue range in to the blue miles. strong,
rested: the thousand horses, the men.

[reel 5]

strong men are reaching-eyed are
riding a thousand horses in the desert

west. are riding horses. horses range-eyed
from the orange miles and miles men, men crying! except
in the too strong west. the too strong west that
the strong men are reaching to. from. the strong
men riding the strong horses, the thousand thousand miles men
are strong in the strong orange desert strong men in the strong west are.

# The Sundays of Satin-Legs Smith

## PATIENCE AGBABI

Patience Agbabi is a sought-after poet, performer, mentor, and fellow in creative writing at Oxford Brookes University. She read English at Oxford and has an MA in creative writing from the University of Sussex. Her fourth collection, *Telling Tales* (Canongate, 2014), is a Canterbury Tales for the twenty-first century.

### Her Secret

Make-up's a mask. She wants to be a he:
to shin up trees, steal speckled eggs from swallows,
strip to the waist in undiluted sunshine.
The kind of boy you'd arm wrestle with
just to get close, a bare-knuckled *what's a
nice girl like you doing with?* Her secret
locked in a grip so firm, it makes them yelp.

## TERI CROSS DAVIS

Teri Cross Davis has attended Cave Canem, the Soul Mountain Writer's Retreat, the Virginia Center for Creative Arts, and the Fine Arts Work Center in Provincetown. Her work has been published in many anthologies and journals including *Bum Rush the Page: A Def Poetry Jam,* and *Poet Lore.*

### One Night Stand

If this is desire, let consumption's
pace leave the body spiritless.
Let the morning's tears be expectoration;
ejecting the ether of guilt, an
absolution of action, flesh indignant
of limits imaginary, arbitrary. Hear the robin's

glory sear the day, resolute
the deed is done. Lust was your donation.

---

## MARTY MCCONNELL

Marty McConnell lives in Chicago, Illinois, and received her MFA from Sarah
Lawrence College. Her work has recently appeared in *Best American Poetry 2014,
Southern Humanities Review, Gulf Coast,* and *Indiana Review.* Her first full-length
collection, *Wine for a Shotgun,* was published in 2012 by EM Press.

### note to the unconceived

I have forgotten you. But
sometimes, laying in wonder
at the distant, lavish night, and suits
lined up on plastic hangers, in
and out of fashion, something yellow
comes to sit with me. And
in that half-dreaming minute, in
the hard permission of the third red wine,
there you are. As you were never: sarcastic,
bodied, laughing. I want to be somewhere green.
Night, day, rust on the machine and
the oil can. I might as well talk about a zebra
as forgetting. Call myself a horse, but striped.
Night not singular, but magnetic, alloyed, cobalt.

---

## EILEEN MYLES

Eileen Myles is the author of nineteen books including *I Must Be Living Twice:
New and Selected Poems* and a re-issue of *Chelsea Girls* from Ecco/Harper Collins
in 2015. She is a recipient of a Guggenheim, a Warhol/Creative Capital grant,
and the Shelly Prize. She lives in New York.

## Hot Water

This evening which the rain is the provider now
keeps me in all day I've been calm at
my desk on my couch and I'm a child of his
when I was ten dad's bath
he asked for a towel sd would
you get me a towel I didn't mean you
should come in here O daddy see deny
yeah don't be angry anything of him
what you had in the tub it was lavender

---

## LAWRENCE RAAB

Lawrence Raab is the author of eight collections of poems including *The History of Forgetting* (Penguin, 2009), *A Cup of Water Turns into a Rose* (Adastra Press, 2012), and *Mistaking Each Other for Ghosts* (Tupelo Press, 2015), which was nominated for the National Book Award. He teaches literature and writing at Williams College.

## Judas

No longer meek and mild, what would He
demand of me, if he came back now? Is
there really nothing in the fat
heart of man that has not changed? *And
what about you, my friend?* he might ask. *How fine
do you feel?* How justified that so much of this
life keeps slipping through your fingers every morning?
Then again at night. And each day thereafter. Definite,
isn't it? Consider yourself paid in full. Reimbursed.

---

## RAVI SHANKAR

Ravi Shankar is an award-winning poet, author, translator, and founding editor of Drunken Boat, who has appeared in the *New York Times* and on NPR and the

BBC. His many books include *Language for a New Century*, *Deepening Groove*, *Instrumentality*, and *What Else Could It Be*.

## The Narcissist Breaks Up

Severe narcissistic personality disorder is what he
tells her when he is about to break up with her. Looks

victimized by his own flaws, tragically submerging into
shallow pools of self-pity, trying his best to hold his

breath underwater & using the sounds as a mirror.
How much anguish is shown in response? He loves

the feeling of having been missed. Alone, by himself,
he savors that feeling. Alone, in his mind, he is not the

misshapen cactus he appears to be in public, too neat,
monastic, deliberate, someone who takes each curve

too slowly. No, when he finds himself alone out here,
he is a family, a voting district represented in the

electoral college, one single hue, all error & angularity
straightened out. Either for or against. Blue/Red. Or is that

a reduction of the situation? Whatever the case, it is
just that he doesn't know what might be most appropriate

to feel when he is numb most of the rest of the time, even at
the most inopportune moments like at weddings, just

like his mother who always drank and made a scene. Its
not right to sanctify the mortal life in such a shit place,

she'd screech pointing wildly at pews, the Bibles & the
crucifix hanging above the bride. The best technique

then was to ignore her, or if that failed to bring a pinch of
sleeping powder to put in her wine. That's why, even a

grown man, he can't return love. Too variegated
for this black & white world, he says. Wish me grace.

---

## DARA WIER

Dara Wier is a professor at the University of Massachusetts, Amherst Program for
Poets and Writers; cofounder and codirector of the Juniper Initiative for Literary
Arts and Action; cofounder and codirector of the Juniper Summer Writing
Institute and Workshops; and publisher and editor of Factory Hollow Press.

### For Gwendolyn Brooks

with it being spring and all, so that
no one doesn't know what time it is, no,
everyone resolves to perfect a performance
as strict as a season, as necessary as may
seems now to April be and to bees to be
the essence of frivolity and gaudy and plain
with sweet notice and careful recognition or
else what she has written has been in vain

# A Sunset of the City

## ELIZABETH BERG

Elizabeth Berg is the *New York Times* best-selling author of twenty novels, two collections of short stories, and two nonfiction works. She submitted her first poem for publication when she was nine, which was promptly rejected. So she is very happy to have the second attempt published here.

### Yard Sale

Unused negligee, silver pie server, pearls with a broken clasp, Whose?
The dishes have been tagged and washed
I hear in the $1.00 teapot the echoes
Of perfumed women in pastel dresses who are
Glad of the chance to be out, tremulous
With the need to talk, to talk; to lay down
Cards, to eat cashews from cut-crystal bowls, all that lost
Joined with those other things gone down long, dark halls.

---

## MAXINE CHERNOFF

Maxine Chernoff is the author of fourteen books of poetry and six works of fiction. A 2013 recipient of an National Endowment for the Arts in Poetry, she also won the 2009 PEN Translation Award and a Gwendolyn Brooks Poet Laureate Award when she lived in Chicago. She is chair of creative writing at San Francisco State University and former editor of *New American Writing*.

The sun had dimmed already
Exposing the soft copper of the self, the I
That stands by the window whispering ' I am'
Without a flagrant word, a yes or no,
For instance, or a sum of words longer

Than time's latitude on the map looked
At by travelers whose ships were at
The harbor, ready to embark, with
Hope and trepidation. What lechery
Can't claim is a singular moment or
The spell one casts, gaudy remedy, lucid as love.

———————

## DANIEL DONAGHY

Daniel Donaghy is the author of two poetry collections, *Start with the Trouble*
(University of Arkansas Press, 2009) and Streetfighting (BkMk Press, 2005).
He is a professor of English at Eastern Connecticut State University.

### Somerset

An El train squeals into Somerset like it
doesn't want to stop, like it knows what is

wilting in its shadows—summer-gone
corner boys, women tricking in bars that
peddle *rock* and *dope*, *weed* and *wet* to guys I

might have known as a child. Somerset, see,
is Zombieland: abandominiums, speedballs to the neck. It

is storefront ministries, pawnshops, no cops. Is
a father's fist, a daughter's scream. Is summer-gone
as the smokestacks and textile mills that spilled the

street's first darkness. Gone as a huckster's sweet
corn, as a widow's flowers

flaming in a window box, as a junkie in drying
in a burned-out car, lost to meth mouth and
swallowed by chest-high weeds. The El knows dying,

knows when to shut its doors. Down
on Somerset, they're dispensing free samples of the

day's best. They're kneeling in alley grasses
denying their sponsors, forgetting
the missionaries who nodded all morning through their

heartbreak and new-start promises. Blaze.
Spoon sizzle. Time screeches still as an El train and

they curl up in God's blanket, consenting
themselves with a ride that will get them only back to
Somerset and their next round of brown.

---

## PERCIVAL EVERETT

Percival Everett is author of novels and collections of short fiction. He is
distinguished professor of English at the University of Southern California.

A circle finds its way and
tautologies circle round this night.
Love is a truth that isn't and is
while tautologies circle round this night.

---

## MARIA MAZZIOTTI GILLAN

Maria Mazziotti Gillan is a recipient of AWP's 2014 George Garrett Award,
Poets and Writers' 2011 Barnes and Noble Writers for Writers Award, and
the 2008 American Book Award. She is founder/executive director of the
Poetry Center at Passaic County Community College and director of creative
writing/professor of English at Binghamton University-State University of
New York.

### In Honor of Gwendolyn Brooks: A Shovel Poem

In this year of grief my
heart lives only in my daughter
the way she brings joy with her and
laughter, lifts my shawl of sorrow; my sons
solid and dependable, closed up like fists, have
left behind all memories, put
them on a dusty shelf they don't look at, me,
a photograph so old it fades away.

––––––––––

### FANNY HOWE

Fanny Howe has published numerous books of fiction, poetry, and essays. She is a recipient of the Ruth Lilly Lifetime Achievement Award and a finalist for the Man Booker International Award in 2015, and her most recent collection of poetry, *Second Childhood* (Greywolf, 2014) was a finalist for the National Book Award.

### Twang they. And I incline this ear to tin.

If my fingers could twang
the guitar as before they
would not be what they are and
neither would I. I
would be back in young-time. Incline
towards me, Gwendolyn, this
Monday, and lend me your ear
while I loll on my pillows to
turn your songs from strings into tin.

––––––––––

### LANGSTON KERMAN

Langston Kerman is a poet, comedian, actor, and teacher hailing from Oak Park, Illinois. He earned his MFA in poetry from Boston University, studying under Robert Pinsky, Louise Gluck, and David Ferry. He now resides in Brooklyn, New York, where he mostly yells silly jokes into a microphone.

## This Feels Permanent

I am hurting the way trees hurt. The
screams hollowed in some fallen philosophy. Grasses
taunt like skeletons. It's been months since you started forgetting.

This must be how trees think of their lumberjack. Yes he is their
murderer. Yes he unwound their rings in a plaid blaze.
Yes he is mostly saw and jagged and spit and

unmoved by bistro tables and hardcovers. Still he is consenting.
I miss you like the dying miss the knife. Please—be anything to
cut through this silence melting into brown.

---

## DORIANNE LAUX

Dorianne Laux is the author of several poetry collections, including *Facts about the Moon*, winner of the Oregon Book Award, and *The Book of Men*, winner of the Paterson Poetry Prize. Laux has received fellowships from the Guggenheim Foundation and the National Endowment for the Arts. She teaches poetry in the MFA program at North Carolina State University and is founding faculty at Pacific University's Low Residency MFA Program.

## Lapse

I am not deceived, I do not think it is still summer. I
see the leaves turning on their stems. I am
not oblivious to the sun as it lowers on its stem, not
fooled by the clock holding off, not deceived
by the weight of its tired hands holding forth. I
do not think my dead will return. They will not do
what I ask of them. Even if I plead on my knees. Not
even if I kiss their photographs or think
of them as I touch the things they left me. It
isn't possible to raise them from their beds, is
it? Even if I push the dirt away with my bare hands? Still-
ness, unearth their faces. Bring me the last dahlias of summer.

## LEE MARTIN

Lee Martin has published three memoirs, most recently, *Such a Life*. He is also the author of four novels, including *Break the Skin* and *The Bright Forever*, a finalist for the 2006 Pulitzer Prize in Fiction. He teaches in the MFA program at the Ohio State University.

## Twig by Twig

A nest in the crabapple; inside, I
watch the robin at work, and I am
holding my breath in the cold
air the open window lets in,
afraid she may fly. Then this
silence will choke me, this cold
morning will undo me. This house
will be walls and roof, this
day. Twig by twig. This house.

## E. ETHELBERT MILLER

E. Ethelbert Miller is a writer and literary activist. He is the author of several collections of poems and two memoirs. Mr. Miller is the board chair of the Institute for Policy Studies. In 2015 he was inducted into the Washington DC Hall of Fame.

## Just a Friend after Sunset

I spoke with her yesterday, she was my
neighbor. At night the city took her husband
leaving tears outside her door and
strange men wanting to be lovers.
I counted myself among them but there are
things I only dream of doing—none pleasant.
In this city after sunset it's neither warm or
cold. I could hide my feelings somewhat
like a gun. To love or kill is not polite.

## KAMILAH AISHA MOON

Kamilah Aisha Moon's work has been featured widely in journals and anthologies. Selected as a New American Poet presented by the Poetry Society of America, a Pushcart Prize winner, and a finalist for the Lambda Literary Award, Moon is the author of *She Has a Name* (Four Way Books).

### Golden Shovel

Bright fields recede to jigsaw pieces as the
plane tugs us closer to heaven, the grasses
uniform from this view, none of us forgetting
how hunger and thirst chain bodies to their
every whim. Oh, how to ignite a soul blaze
that doesn't require sustained burning and
ash clearing, the caresses of two consenting
adults to sanction an impossible ceremony—to
bless the searing green of it all, and the brown.

The wrong ghost beckons me by name to come:
she wants me to lean into arms that aren't there,
to find solace in thin air. *Que sera sera, what shall
be shall be.* Damn, so much woman unable to be
solid or certain in any way, her earth-toned skin such
a ruse. Despite a continent of memories, islanding
those misspent years proves brutal to recover from,
winnowing wisdom from stubborn grains of grief.

## NII AYIKWEI PARKES

Winner of multiple international awards including Ghana's Arts Critics and Reviewers Association Award and France's Prix Laure Bataillon, Nii Ayikwei Parkes is the author of *Tail of the Blue Bird* (novel), and *The Makings of You* (poetry). In 2014 he was selected as one of Africa's thirty-nine most promising authors of the new generation.

## Awaiting Dawn

Twilight's first breath is with us. Already
the year turns like a lathe and still I am
no more than my father's son, no longer
gone from my youth than the last time I peeked.

But I have come to know where the wisdom's at,
which stones it lies beneath, what winds it myths with;
I reach for it across dawn's skein, with casual lechery,
distilled need. It tells me nothing of death or love.

---

## LINDA PASTAN

Linda Pastan has written fourteen books of poetry, most recently *Insomnia*. She
was twice a finalist for the National Book Award and in 2003 won the Ruth Lilly
Award for lifetime achievement. She was poet laureate of Maryland and was on
the staff of the Bread Loaf Writer's Conference for twenty years.

## One Day Soon

One day soon the long grasses
will cover us both, forgetting
how we planted the seed for their
silky spikes, how the blaze
of their green has to be watered and
cut, and watered again, how consenting
to our ordinary deaths, they too,
as they blanket us, will fade to brown.

---

## KATHLEEN ROONEY

Kathleen Rooney is a founding editor of Rose Metal Press and a founding
member of Poems While You Wait. Her most recent book is the novel
*O, Democracy!*, and she is the co-editor of *Rene Magritte: Selected Writings*,
forthcoming from Alma Books in 2016.

## American Realness

The business of America? They say it
is business. Anyone who sells is
going to be liked. The opposite, a
corollary, is equally true. Real
successes never sunset, never just chill.
Corsaged and peroxided, they go out
in their cities night after night. The
light in their faces the next day is genuine,
even if their coffee isn't working at anything.

—————

## FIONA SAMPSON

Fiona Sampson has published twenty books, including books of poetry,
volumes on the philosophy of language, and on the writing process. Her
poetry has been broadcast and published in over thirty languages. She has won
the Cholmondeley Award (2009), the 2003 Zlaten Prsten for international
writing (Macedonian Foundation for Culture and Sciences), a Hawthornden
Fellowship, the Newdigate Prize, and awards from the Arts Councils of
England and Wales and the Society of Authors. She is professor of poetry at
Roehampton University.

## Travel Literature

All night the trains thunder. Whose
stories are those, racing away, washed
clean by the dark? Their echoes
disturb, disturb, disturb . . . Stories are what we are—

bravado, or the tremulous
fantasy in which we too disappear down
those tracks, until we're lost
and find ourselves in far arrival halls.

## MARTHA SERPAS

Martha Serpas is the author of *Côte Blanche, The Dirty Side of the Storm,* and *The Diener.* Her work is featured in *Veins in the Gulf,* an internationally screened documentary about Louisiana's disappearing coast. She teaches in the creative writing program at the University of Houston and is a hospital trauma chaplain.

### Funland

Family Funland awaits us. Come:
let's hit the fast track there,
perfuming us with gas fumes, we shall
race ghostly go-karts, be
challenged to keep them such
a distance, on the Gulf Stream, islanding
from each other, from
the final lap's cut-engine grief.

## LEE UPTON

Lee Upton's sixth collection of poetry, *Bottle the Bottles the Bottles the Bottles,* appeared in 2015 from the Cleveland State University Poetry Center. Her collection of short stories, *The Tao of Humiliation,* was selected as one of the "best books of 2014" by *Kirkus Reviews,* received the BOA Short Fiction Award, and was a finalist for the Paterson Prize. She is the Francis A. March Professor of English and writer-in-residence at Lafayette College.

### Already

Words cannot help. Already
I've lost whatever I wanted, and I
know better than to think that what I am
is going to be found through words. No
matter where I turn the nights are longer
and others turn away from where I once looked.
Should it matter? The benches fill with snow at

the park's center, the paths slicken with
ice. The old words—gluttony, avarice, lechery—
slide away and new words cannot take their place. Or
is it only this?: I'm not ready to be embarrassed, again, already, by love.

---

## JULIE MARIE WADE

Julie Marie Wade is the author of eight collections of poetry and prose, including
*When I Was Straight: Poems* (A Midsummer Night's Press, 2014) and *Wishbone: A
Memoir in Fractures* (Bywater Books, 2014; Colgate University Press, 2010). She
teaches in the creative writing program at Florida International University
in Miami.

### Avow

How can it be already
twelve years that I
have not been able to stand as I am
at the altar beside you? *Yes, no,*
*maybe so,* the laws go, longer
the appeals to Heaven than reason. We looked
before we leapt, while strangers gaped at
our falling. We wove our story tightly with
two pairs of women's hands. This is not lechery,
or madness, or temptation, or
disease. This is merely the marriage of a more-than-decade's love.

---

## DANIELLE ZIPKIN

Danielle Zipkin began writing poetry in the founding class of Peter Kahn's
Spoken Word Pedagogy graduate program during her time in Chicago as a Teach
For America corps member. She now teaches humanities, drama, and spoken
word in the New York City public schools.

## Cold Sore

Shower water stormed my shoulders more lightly than your put(ting)
Refusals spiraled through my ear gutters. My eyes followed yours to the me(an)
Sore my lip wore at its corner like a red fascinator, like a (run)away
Fish egg ripe for hatching, like a pregnant volcano, like the one you caught
    with(out)
Symptom from the well of your colleague's crusty mouth. It marbles
Your vision of my face-before-kiss, so you knuckle-down the shower knob, and
Towel-hug me dry with a smile cut for function like a plastic dolls'.

# Throwing Out the Flowers

## ELEANOR WILNER

Eleanor Wilner's most recent books are *Tourist in Hell* (University of Chicago) and *The Girl with Bees in Her Hair* (Copper Canyon Press). A forever fan of Gwendolyn Brooks, she teaches in the MFA Program for Writers at Warren Wilson College.

### Over and Over and All

Such a long slow stream leads to the
place in the reeds where the duck
hides her eggs, thick shells sheltering the rich fats
within that feed the unborn, in the wet rot
that cushions the nest safely tucked in
the reeds like Moses in his basket in the
old tale, boy about to be lifted into the roasting
sun, wrapped in Egyptian cotton—slow pan

across the ages, following the Nile, *now* and
*then* in a single frame, time's transit of its
long collective memory, a story told over
and over (the rescue, the turning against) and
the hawk swooping . . . it's about to be over
before the hatching, her useless flurry and
beating of wings—all her eggs broken—all

her pretty ones, undone. And the daughter of the
Pharaoh, God's pawn, lonely in the stone halls, the fine
linens, the long sun-struck afternoons, fraught
with a girl's dreams, where the beguiling smiles
of the servants are as false as the promises and
prayers of the priests, plotting, filled with spites,
sealing the women alive in the tombs that

house the *fellahin's* hope of another life. What began
     before
in a different time, another place, echoes in the call: it
rose skyward among the cotton rows; it was
the oldest cry: *let my people go*, and before it was over
(is it ever over?), promises broken like heads and
     like eggs—the hawks circling over and over us all.

# To An Old Black Woman, Homeless, and Indistinct

## YONA HARVEY

Yona Harvey is the author of *Hemming the Water,* winner of the Kate Tufts Discovery Award. She lives in Pittsburgh, Pennsylvania.

### Necessarily

She's got a hundred & two temperature, delivery room nurses said. You're
gonna live, though—long enough to know you're going
to go as quickly as you came, gonna make your mother swear by you, going to
shake your Bible with red-tipped nails before you vanish
into Chicago South Side skies that bleed—not like watercolor, not like a wound, not
like a fat, bitten plum—not necessarily. No, not necessarily.
Nothing that precious or predictable. Speak nicely to others & they will nicely
speak to you, your mother said. No, not so, you said fairly
close to the end. No time to wait for mother's ride home or for saviors, coming soon.

# To Be In Love

## JULIA GLASS

Julia Glass is the author of five books of fiction: *And the Dark Sacred Night, The Widower's Tale, I See You Everywhere, The Whole World Over,* and *Three Junes.* Her honors include a National Book Award, a Binghamton University John Gardner Award, and fellowships from the National Endowment for the Arts and the Radcliffe Center for Advanced Study.

### Two Poems for Alec

1. Checklist of Expectations

Bedroom vacant, piano silent, a little less laundry to
do: Check. Everyone asking me how it feels: Check. The sense of be-
reftness, waking to the phantom-limb certainty you are upstairs, still in
bed, sleeping later than you should: Check. The recurrent swell of my love

for you, more often and ardent because the only thing to complain about is
your neglect, your apparent (and I am told perfectly normal) refusal to
even pretend that you miss us: Roger that! (Staying in touch
is our deal.) But this one—me writing torrents of old-fashioned letters, assailing
    you with
reminders of home—is not checked. Oh yes, I want more, but not you looking
    over a
shoulder, turning around *too* much. What I did not expect: to strive for a lighter
touch in loving you, the same touch your piano—also bereft—taught your
    growing hand.

2. Divergence

We knew this day would arrive . . . and you depart. You
are the one who yearned it, dreamed it, schemed it. You are
the one who stepped off, I the one who waved. Predictable now, the

pull of the past, holding me back, just a moment, from the risky, beautiful,
double-dare-you-and-dare-me-too future, now split. So take your half

and go your distance while I go mine. I zigzag to and fro through landscapes of
ages and stages, songs and rages, leaps and falls. As if through the window of a
   Golden
speeding train, I glimpse forest-meadow-river-city, brightness-shadow-pride-regret.
Countries hurtle by. To travel is to gather but also to part; sometimes the distances
   hurt.

———————

## MAURA SNELL

Maura Snell is cofounder and poetry editor at *The Tishman Review*, and teaches
poetry writing and critique to incarcerated teen girls. Her work can be found
both online and in print, most recently at *Brain, Child Magazine*. Check out
essays, book reviews, and other material at www.thetishmanreview.com.

### Hotel Lobby, April Evening

His hands cup her stomach as she sits on his lap. She leans in. You
blur my bones. Even from this distance, our bodies remember.

His face is not yours, nor her hips mine, but they become you and
me. And I'm hungry. I sip my wine. I covet

the language of those fingertips, his stubble, her earlobe. His
thigh, her back, his eyes, her lips. His open mouth.

———————

## TONY TRIGILIO

Tony Trigilio's recent poetry collections are *The Complete "Dark Shadows" (of
My Childhood), Book 1* (BlazeVOX Books, 2014) and *White Noise* (Apostrophe
Books, 2013). He is editor of *Elise Cowen: Poems and Fragments* (Ahsahta Press,
2014). He hosts the monthly poetry podcast *Radio Free Albion* and plays in the
band Pet Theories. He is interim chair of the Department of Creative Writing at
Columbia College Chicago.

## To Be in Love

I'm wiping the glass like a magician waving to
the crowd before he makes it disappear, be-

guiled downtown on the elevated. Spectacular in
the sky in chrome. Tinnitus burns the eardrum, love

makes everything louder than everything else. Is
this only footstomps in the chest? Or a caress, to

grace the sliding door with pristine glove? Don't touch.
Out the window, shapes in a rusty rail-tower, things

fished from shipwreck documentaries shot with
grave voiceover. We're holding each other on a

train suspended above the Loop. Lighter and lighter,
this floating world, miles of track in your open hand.

# To Black Women

## SHARON G. FLAKE

Sharon G. Flake's break-out novel *The Skin I'm In* sealed her place among the top novelists for youth in the world. A multiple Coretta Scott King Award winner, her work appears in several languages, including Korean, French, and Portuguese. Her books have been included on such lists as Best Books of the Year; Top Ten Book of the Year, and 100 Best Books for the Feminist Reader.

She never saw life as hard
no long black walk or trudge
for them willing to work with
no complaint or fainting
but then the storms pulled off her bandaging
bloodying her assets and
showing scabs that long ago warned of death.

# To the Young Who Want to Die

## BOB HICOK

Bob Hicok's eighth book, *Sex & Love &*, was published by Copper Canyon Press in 2016.

## Oath

I can't get over how badly we treat graves
when we bring them flowers that can only grow
deader—you'd think when we were kids, no
one taught us manners—to wipe our feet—that green
is a kiss not to be taken for granted—so trust that,
if you go first, I'll become the gardener you
probably should have married—quiet—weathered—a man who can
touch the earth to bloom—and put the dead to living use

# Truth

## CAMARA BROWN

Camara Brown attends the University of Pennsylvania where she studies urban studies, creative writing, and political Science and is a member of The Excelano Project, a spoken word poetry group. In high school, she received a silver medal in the Scholastic Arts and Writing competition. She also has competed in various poetry slams and won the Berkley (California) Slam.

### What I would ask of Manman Brigitte* after seeing the African Burial Ground†

How long does it take to reclaim a sweet
soul? Does a gentle-palmed boy go quick? Is
a man with dry hair and vulgar tongue not have what it
takes to move on? What if it has no name or any sign to
its legs? What if we can't tell anymore? Do they sleep
far from the hull of this black granite? Do they lie in
sheets of black night with the others? Is there a chance the
newborn souls slid out before their 24 foot burial? What coolness
did their cheeks feel when rising through the rubble of
prehistoric epic centers and City Halls? Were you surprised how snug
they tucked them under the concrete, how horrendous the unawareness?

———

*Manman Brigette is the female cemetery guardian and helps reclaim the souls of the dead. She is the wife of Baron Samedi in Vodou. She is known to drink rum and use obscenities.

———

† The African Burial Ground National Monument memorializes the 419 bodies of Africans found buried under lower Manhattan. Free Africans and African slaves used 6.6 acres of Manhattan to bury their dead. For over two centuries, Wall Street, City Hall, and New York City built itself on top of those remains. Now, 3.4 acres of that land is devoted to remembering them.

## INUA ELLAMS

Inua Ellams is a poet, playwright, performer, graphic artist, and designer. Identity, displacement, and destiny are reoccurring themes in his work, where he tries to mix the old with the new: traditional storytelling with contemporary poetry / pencil with pixel / texture with vector. His books are published by Flipped Eye, Akashic, and Oberon.

## No apps for sunlight

And should the sun abscond from the west, neither yell What
with question marks for eyes, nor stand there stupefied as if
why it favours the east is any wonder. Just imagine, were we
to tirelessly feed the whole solar system—Earth, to ever wake
and work its continent-sized fields, I'm talking every tiny one
emerald twinkle of a shoot, each bee, each river-shimmering
and each groggy wrist reaching for pale screens each morning
—their pathetic lights so unworthy a thing to first turn to.

## CHRIS HAVEN

Chris Haven's poetry has appeared in journals including *Beloit Poetry Journal*, *Pleiades*, *Colorado Review*, and *Seneca Review*. He teaches writing at Grand Valley State University in Michigan and has recently finished a novel, *Frail My Heart*.

## The dark hangs heavily

I have taken to calling the darkness sweet.
It is the way I keep it out. It is
the swish of broomstraw across the floor. It
is a lonely sound only if you forget how sweet.
Just a little taste will tell you how it is.
But must you? Child, you don't want to taste it.
You don't want to let it inside you, to
open your mouth to the darkness, let it sleep
on your tongue. It will lie there, in

a ball where it can't be caught, tricked by the
lie of how sweet it is, by the coolness
of the space around it, the coolness of
its own hate. Hate wants to sleep, sound and snug,
curled in the dark of your unawareness.

----

## ELLEN DORÉ WATSON

Poet and translator Ellen Doré Watson is author of four books, most recently
*Dogged Hearts*. She serves as director of the Poetry Center at Smith College, is the
poetry and translation editor of *Massachusetts Review*, and teaches on the faculty
of the Colrain Manuscript Conference and the Drew University Low-Residency
MFA Program.

## True & False

Creatures don't experience simultaneous *eager* and
*unready*. Does the swift-tawny gazelle even *know* eager, if
she's a gazelle—not a woman who craves savannah and sun,
or thinks so, despite inner-unraveled, her need for dark. Comes
first hint of light, she tunnels under, insists night linger, wonders how
ever to shine, wonder undermining, head hammering: how shall
I approach tender tenderly, ever—much less tiptoe toward *we*,
when bare means naked means fear, means no means to greet.
Despite deep flutter, she means—true & false—to meet him.

----

## INDIGO WILLIAMS

Indigo Williams has performed her spoken word poetry on BBC Radio 4's
*Bespoken Word*, Tedx Brixton, at the Glastonbury Festival and the Cheltenham
Literature Festival. She has facilitated workshops across Europe, Bangladesh, and
Nigeria. She is a spoken-word educator working full-time in a secondary school
as part of the pioneering Spoken Word Educators program in conjunction with
Goldsmiths University.

## Truth

Sister, let us pretend we are ribbon haired girls again and
that our bodies sing to us instead of men. Come, maybe if
we try hard enough we will remember a song or a sun
before catcalls or boys that stalk with good intentions. It comes
back to me sometimes, the child body, smooth and free, how
I made angels with waving limbs. This poem's wings shall
send us skirts parachuting back to the green, green grass we
loved on our backs. Sister, let us pretend the world is safe. Greet
every strange man with lemonade and pick daisies. For Him?

# The Vacant Lot

## SUE DYMOKE

Sue Dymoke's second full collection is *Moon at the Park and Ride* (Shoestring Press, 2012,). She is reader in education and National Teaching Fellow at the University of Leicester, United Kingdom, where she researches poetry pedagogy (see Sue Dymoke, Myra Barrs, Andrew Lambirth, and Anthony Wilson, *Making Poetry Happen*, Bloomsbury, 2015). Sue blogs at suedymokepoetry.com.

### The Way He Lived Now

She knew there was trouble with
the way he lived now when she ventured into his
garden again, saw the creeping speedwell, great
purple thistles instead of bean poles, white
dead-head nettles colonising borders with their strong
nicotine-fingered roots and the empty cold
frames where seedlings in serried squares
once waited for the next stage of
propagation but she could only pull weeds, grit her teeth.

---

## PHILIP GROSS

Philip Gross is professor of creative writing at the University of South Wales, United Kingdom. He won the British T. S. Eliot Prize for 2009 with *The Water Table. A Fold in the River,* with artist Valerie Coffin Price, appeared in 2015, as did a new collection *Love Songs of Carbon* (Bloodaxe Books). www.philipgross. co.uk.

### Memento Mori

The man stripped bare, the man beneath,
                    the one you least want to be with . . .
Cover his tracks for all you're worth
                    for fear you can't tell which are his

and which your own. You know he has
                    a place for you, here, in his great
vacant lot, just *so* wide. Grit
                    leaks in, mould-shadow on the white
walls: all home comforts, what
                    more could you want? That and a strong
suspicion that you've *been* here. Strung
                    with wind, he hums along. He's the cold
ocarina on which . . . what's it called,
                    that tune? busks alone in the echoing squares.
For any later stranger who enquires,
                    he has the lowdown—lasting witness of
the way you live, eat, fight and love:
                    his worn, or filled, or missing teeth.

---

## FRANCINE J. HARRIS

francine j. harris is a 2015 National Endowment for the Arts fellow whose first collection, *allegiance*. She was a finalist for both the Kate Tufts Discovery Award and the PEN Open Book Award. Her second book, *Play Dead*, is forthcoming from Alice James Books. Originally from Detroit, she is writer in residence at Washington University in St. Louis.

## The Lot, Vacant Then

When I dug the bare trench, I did it with twigs and
flung in our bones, both sets, both heads, and called you king with
my candy fish and peppermint sticks, while you stood across the street seeing
my vatic branch in hand and my sugar blushed cheeks, and you held out the
paper gold crown and kicked, and watched it land, and had I sat squat
beneath it, bull body in dirt for wedding, with baby fat
of want and weather, had I been the daughter
that didn't breathe it, didn't prop it in feather, never letting
you touch me in hedgerow, or snick me in
rag, how might mud have first shivered, the
cast we opened, before men

lifted my skirts when
I let them in eyelets, with cardboard majesty
digging ditch with sticks in empty lot that has
rent away rebar and buried what's gone
of your worry, and what if we looked for
the minelay, snuck back to black curls against the
kingdom, blue dawn the bare branch, which day
would bare our blank horizon, like trellis we'd stand
castle under, fingers laced in slat, letting
no one else name it, no ground for any of them
to hush and condemn, and move us out
from, our mouths red with dirt again.

# We Real Cool

## MARY CALVIN

Mary Calvin lives in Portland, Oregon, with her husband, John, and small dog, Chester. She writes, volunteers as a docent at the Portland Art Museum, and studies the piano. Her work has been published in *CALYX Journal*.

### 1950: Norco, Louisiana

The news knifes through the air and we
clamber down from our perch in the oak tree, the real
world having shattered the imaginary with one cool
thrust through summer's humidity. Later we

ride together to the wake, the levee on our left,
in the opposite direction we normally take to school
when our world is not disrupted by a tragedy we
cannot comprehend. Questions stir then lurk

in wordless disarray as we toss in our beds late
at night before the screech owl pierces our dreams. We
stand in line for the viewing. The three coffins strike
out across the room, head to toe, like a path straight

into a moss-hung cypress swamp with no exit. We
look down on the three brothers who will no longer sing
and who were too young to be burdened with sin.
Their hair must have grown longer in death, we

notice. We nod to our friend, her family now thinned
to three daughters and one son because a gin
drunk driver hit the rest head on. Even at ten, we
talk predestination—how else to explain how two Jazz

teammates and their bat-boy brother found themselves one June
night in the bull's eye of the drunk as he crossed the line. We
wonder how death will come for us. Will it be violent? Will we die
in our beds? Will fate be that cruel to take us too soon?

————————

## STUART DISCHELL

Stuart Dischell's most recent book is *Backwards Days* (Penguin). His first two
collections *Good Hope Road* (winner of the 1993 National Poetry Series) and
*Evenings and Avenues* are being reissued by Carnegie Mellon University Press
in their Contemporary Classics Series. He teaches in the MFA program at the
University of North Carolina at Greensboro.

### Parisian Shuffle

Never a chance for me to say *oui*
Or *non* in this town that invented surreal,
I can only respond, "Cool,"
When you text this morning that we
Can meet each other after Claude has left
For work and Mathilde has gone to school.

\*


Drinks in the morning. Even a wee
Cocktail is not healthy as I lurk
In my window, waiting for you, always late.
I pray there is a chance that we
Will be *sur la piste* before the church bells strike.
I will never get you straight.

\*


Mostly past and with little future, we
Long for the present. Your letters sing
When you say the word sin
With an accent only a sinner can. We

Have rules for putting together our thin
Selves once more with juice and gin.

\*

Is only you and I. Never we.
You want the blues and I want jazz.
Our bodies measure every June.
In bed we rock to *ouais* and *oui*.
The horn fades out and the drums die.
You say sometime and I say soon.

---

## CAMILLE T. DUNGY

Camille T. Dungy is the author of three books, most recently *Smith Blue*, and has edited three more, including *Black Nature: Four Centuries of African American Nature Poetry*. Her honors include an American Book Award, two Northern California Book Awards, and an National Endowment for the Arts grant. Dungy teaches at Colorado State University.

### Because it looked hotter that way

we let our hair down. It wasn't so much that we
worried about what people thought or about keeping it real
but that we knew this was our moment. We knew we'd blow our cool

sooner or later. Probably sooner. Probably even before we
got too far out of Westmont High and had kids of our own who left
home wearing clothes we didn't think belonged in school.

Like Mrs. C. whose nearly unrecognizably pretty senior photo we
passed every day on the way to Gym, we'd get old. Or like Mr. Lurk
who told us all the time how it's never too late

to throw a Hail Mary like he did his junior year and how we
could win everything for the team and hear the band strike
up a tune so the cheer squad could sing our name, too. Straight

out of a Hallmark movie, Mr. Lurk's hero turned teacher story. We
had heard it a million times. Sometimes he'd ask us to sing
with him, *T-O-N-Y-L-U-R-K Tony Tony Lurk Lurk Lurk. Sin*

*ironia, con sentimiento, por favor*, and then we
would get back to our Spanish lessons, opening our thin
textbooks, until the bell rang and we went on to the cotton gin

in History. Really, this had nothing to do with being cool. We
only wanted to have a moment to ourselves, a moment before Jazz
Band and after Gym when we could look in the mirror and like it. June

and Tiffany and Janet all told me I looked pretty. We
took turns saying nice things, though we might just as likely say, Die
and go to hell. Beauty or hell. No difference. The bell would ring soon.

———————

## JOY HARJO

> Joy Harjo is an acclaimed poet, musician, writer, and performer. Her eight books
> of award-winning poetry include *She Had Some Horses* and her newest, *Conflict
> Resolution for Holy Beings*. Her awards include the William Carlos Williams
> Award from the Poetry Society of America, and a Guggenheim Fellowship.
> She is at work on a musical and a memoir.

### An American Sunrise

We were running out of breath, as we ran out to meet ourselves. We
were surfacing the edge of our ancestors' fights, and ready to Strike
it was difficult to lose days in the Indian bar if you were Straight.
Easy if you played pool and drank to remember to forget. We
made plans to be professional—and did. And some of us could Sing
so we drummed a fire lit pathway up to those starry stars. Sin
was invented by the Christians, as was the Devil, we sang. We
were the heathens, but needed to be saved from them: Thin
chance. We knew we were all related in this story, a little Gin
will clarify the dark, and make us all feel like dancing. We
had something to do with the origins of blues and Jazz

I argued with a Pueblo as I filled the jukebox with dimes in June,
forty years later and we still want justice. We are still America. We
know the rumors of our demise. We spit them out. They Die Soon.

---

## EDWARD HIRSCH

Edward Hirsch, a Chicago native and MacArthur Fellow, has published nine
books of poems, including *Gabriel: A Poem* (2014), a book-length elegy for
his son, and five books of prose, most recently *A Poet's Glossary* (2014), a full
compendium of poetic terms.

### As Young Poets in Chicago
We followed her through the neighborhood, we
immersed ourselves in her code of the Real,
we booked ourselves into her school.

---

## ELLEN HOPKINS

Ellen Hopkins is a poet and the award-winning author of eleven bestselling
young-adult novels in verse, plus three novels for adults. She lives near Carson
City, Nevada, with her family, two dogs, one cat, and two ponds of koi.

### How Cool Are We?
Arrogant in our gilded ignorance, we
deny, shutter our eyes to the too real
presence of evil, slithering, toad cool

infiltrating our lives. Fathomless, we
lose taste for discourse, no words left
but the vitriol and rhetoric we school

our children in. Into the shadows we
have been drawn, and there we lurk
great whites on shallow shoals, late

to the feed. Hungering, agitated, we
circle, home in on ready prey, strike
without compassion, shoot straight

for the fear pulse. Blood spurts. We
slurp it in, rise up on all fours, sing
of our evolution, flaunt devout sin

trumpeting cast-iron salvation. We
bloat this planet to tilting, then thin
the swell, overdosing on poppy, gin

and steak. Gluttonous with hate, we
mute torture with mood music jazz
Gershwin above low rustles of June

and as screams wilt to whimpers we
swoon, wait for the last strains to die
away. Content sleep will take us soon.

_____

## GAHL LIBERZON

Gahl Liberzon is a writer, performer, and educator living in Chicago, Illinois,
and author of the book, *Bodies, Bodies, Bodies, Bodies, Bodies* (Red Beard Press,
2012). An alumnus of the University of Michigan, Gahl was captain of the
University of Michigan Slam Team and coach for the Ann Arbor Youth Slam
Team.

## The Old NZ

As far as two amateur pool players went we
weren't half bad. Cue tips always busted, bodies real
warped from the younger kids trying to play cool

who swung them like swords or leaned on them like canes. Still, we
learned the rudiments of English: when the line was clear, we'd shoot left
of center and the cue ball would bank just short of pocket, school

the noobs where they stood jawing. Ben and me, we
played every weekend during the concerts, lurked
in the shadows like we were things that went bump late

at night. It was almost true; even though we
both started at CHS, Ben got expelled for his first strike
on the boy who tried to box him out, got ass whooped, then went straight

for the gun and pistol whipped him. We used to beatbox back then too: we
would post up on the first floor ledge, cypher for blazehead emcees or sing
Muddy Waters and freestyle blues while Ben noodled riffs smooth as sin

on an open G-tuned steel body with a socket slide. I felt like we
were two of a kind, even though anyone could see I was too thin
for golden gloves, too butterfingered for guitar, too spastic for the gin

and kool-aid afterparties where guys like Ben got laid. Still, we
had in common a certain faith in what the notes could put in us, the same jazz
that made us practice trick shots every saturday night from august to june,

as if with enough stocked up cool, we could handle any heavy. We
were untested—hadn't watched a single of our friends die
yet. No matter. We'd get cured of that freshness soon.

---

## TYLER MILLS

Tyler Mills is the author of *Tongue Lyre* (Southern Illinois University Press, 2013), winner of the 2011 Crab Orchard Series in Poetry First Book Award. Her poems have appeared in *The New Yorker*, *Poetry*, *Believer*, and the *Boston Review*. She is assistant professor of English at New Mexico Highlands University.

## Hansel in College

I did not believe in a "we":
only you, smoking in the street, hardly real.
*I put that thought in your mind,* you said, the cool
brown of your eyes too round. We

were two stone lions, one with a closed mouth. You left
your apartment open. One wrinkled shirt on a hanger. School
locked you out again. We locked you out. We
thought we saw you in my old car. It was up to me to lurk
outside & count your lead of five white stones. Too late.
Besides that time you scissored my dolls, we
did not fight. I'd follow you to the park. One strike
& you're out. Once you punched me straight
in the mouth. But I hit you first. Sunday is the person we
don't wake for anymore, but I heard you sing
for her in church: a heartbeat early, you said, *Joy.* Sin
does not belong here, a word we
rip out like hair from the drain, a thin
rope of water splashing through it. We stole gin
from our father. We sat on the floor. We
explained the faces in the window, the jazz
hitting the door. I blamed you all June
that the voices spoke to you. I did not believe we
could see the same trees: yours filled with pigeons that die
in sleep, in a tingle in the ear. In a word like *soon.*

_____

## DOROTHY MOORE

Dorothy Moore is a student at Macalester College, studying geography,
education, and urban studies. She has been writing poetry since age fourteen,
when poetry looked a lot like journal writing. She hopes to be a teacher in order
to provide students with the opportunity to find their voices.

## Cool Kids

On the frisbee next to a bed you slept in, we
watch your ex-lover cut lines of coke, real
thin, as if he is parting the sea, neat & cool

strips of white. It is a Friday night and we
have nothing to do but this. Once you left
this bed with your body in your hands, a school-

ing in what it feels like not to be loved. We
are just kids, maybe, girls who crave the lurk
of a night street, boys who come home too late.

Why do you think of your mother as we
glide between the bodies like snakes to strike?
Your body is anything but yours, your ribs straight

bolts of wire. You want to leave you. We
are learning how to bury our old skins, to sing
too loud. How easy it is to forget your sin

in the morning. How easy it would be if we
took too much, you wild thing, you girl thin
as the line, skipping your turn. He pours you gin

straight-up and says *relax, baby, you know we
are just playing.* You hear your heart shake a jazz
ache, blue as the hair in your nose. The june-

juice bowl is empty, your ex-lover is asleep, we
are out of things to do. We are too cool to die.
The stale breath of light comes too soon.

---

SHARON OLDS

## Thanks to Miss Brooks

Thank you for The
mirror you hold up to me, the pool
I thought was for swimming, the players
I thought played cards. When I was Seven
I got my own room, with twin beds, and at
night my mother would come in and lie on me in the
bed and pray. I didn't know that could be sung—Golden

was my home state, in which my family
buried no one with any but a private Shovel

—————

## HALEY PATAIL

Haley Patail graduated with a degree in creative writing from the University
of Michigan, where she won multiple Hopwood Awards for poetry. She is the
coauthor of the poetry collection *Electric Bite Women* from Red Beard Press.
She is currently living, working, reading, and writing in New York City.

## The Golden Shovel (to bury the ghost)

*After Gwendolyn Brooks, Terrance Hayes, and Ben Alfaro*

do you remember the time we
switched places so you got to be the real
one? don't forget me, the taloned cool

on your neck. you go, still awe-
d by what body there is left
to starve. out behind the school

there's a village of your teeth. we
can't all be a house where want lurk-
s like a pulse on skin. late-

ly I sing you to sleep. we
both pretend you don't hear me. I strike
the ground hard, good straight

line of shovel into some we
-alth and weight of dirt. lately I sing
to the worms pushing far as sin

away from you, gaunt sewe-
d up doll of leaves, growing thin
and thinner still. begin-

ning some rattling prayer we
can't finish between us, too muddled with jazz
and anxious the way the night in june

is anxious with moths. you make a good we-
apon out of your hunger. but we both die
if you sharpen your shell too fast, too soon

---

## KADIJA SESAY

Kadija Sesay is an award winning literary activist, publisher of *SABLE LitMag*, and editor of numerous anthologies. Her books include her poetry collection *Irki* (Peepal Tree, 2013), and *21 February: Progress and Possibilities for a Pan Africanism Future* (WoW, 2015) as well as the forthcoming *Modern Pan Africanist's Journey*. She is the TECHNE/AHRC funded PhD scholar researching black independent publishers at Brighton University.

### Kriolising Kulcha

| Kushe Kushe | We real cool. We |
| ustem yu cam me pikin | Left school. We |
| | |
| wori fo yu-o! Lef fo | Lurk late. We |
| sen fo yu mama | Strike straight. We |
| | |
| sen fo yu papa | Sing sin. We |
| pray hard for una | Thin gin. We |
| | |
| no wan mek plaba | Jazz June. We |
| gefo mek gladi tide. | Die soon. |

## MAGS WEBSTER

Mags Webster's first book *The Weather of Tongues* won Australia's Anne Elder Award for a debut collection of poetry. She has an MFA from City University of Hong Kong, and has just started a PhD in creative writing in Western Australia.

### Jessie from the Golden Shovel

It's dawn. Dirty light brings us into focus, the pit where we
shared blood and skin dissolves into a bed again, sheds its surreal
armour. Your shoulders pinch into the pillows, sheets that are cool

at last, again. Almost erased by sleep, I look at you in awe.
The fading tan, the trace of last month's scars, the soft cleft
at the base of your spine. The mouth which gave commands, was school

ma'am stern, then wavered as the night grew cruel. What were we
in that dark? We're not those beings now, the morning's washed the lurk
and shadow from the room, but I can still see bruises—they dilate

like hungry flowers. This is the time of day I like best, before we
humans grow a carapace; we're still naked and unshelled, yet to strike
out of our night-selves. It's when I'm likely to be truthful, and straight-

away, you wake. Your eyes film me, they track and bring me close-up. We
are unrehearsed, we don't know what to do, so we start kissing, kissing
like we're being paid—or I'm the mark and you're the irresistible assassin.

How damned natural it feels. And yet I hardly know you—first time we
hooked up, you left without telling me your name. Tall, blonde, too thin,
you were my abyss. Did you know how much I'd crave you? How I'd begin

to haunt the Shovel, spinning out the gins as long as I dared? And how are we
again? the barman Milt would ask, as again I described you, down to the jazz
tattoo on the back of your shin. That sounds like Jessie, 'cept she OD'd last June.

Who are you, woman in my bed? One thing's for sure, you'll never owe
me anything. Not even your name. So what if you're really dead? We all die
sometime, the cliché goes, and I'm on my way—I'll be there soon. Real soon.

————————

## SHOLEH WOLPÉ

Sholeh Wolpé is a poet and writer. She was born in Iran and lived in Trinidad
and the United Kingdom before settling in the United States. She is the recipient
of the 2014 PEN/Heim, 2013 Midwest Book Award and 2010 Lois Roth Persian
Translation prize. Her nine books include *Keeping Time with Blue Hyacinths*, and
a contemporary translation of Attar's *The Conference of the Birds*, forthcoming
from W. W. Norton in 2017.

### We, the Basij

We,
who cling to air, learned Heaven was real,
martyrdom was cool.

We,
who learned behind crumbling walls right was not left,
memorized God's fierce judgment at school.

We,
who started young—at mosques we'd lurk—
swallowed the chewed morsels of doctrines of late.

We,
now the ninjas of the streets, swing batons to strike
anyone who strays, even snow, from the moral straight.

We,
of the virtuous leaf-colored turbans, sing
*God is Great*—those not with us, are of mortal sin.

We,
who starve depraved women and leftists thin,
shoot all the godless sellers of bathtub gin.

We,
knee and head, savage shut forbidden tunes, jazz,
the half-broken saxophone-wound moaning *Love in June.*

We,
yes we, enforce morality, imbecility—conceal, obey or die.
Or else: we know your human roots, where you live: See you soon.

# When You Have Forgotten Sunday: The Love Story

## BRENDA HILLMAN

Brenda Hillman has published nine collections of poetry with Wesleyan University Press, including *Seasonal Works with Letters on Fire* (2013). With Garrett Caples and Paul Ebenkamp, she coedited Richard O. Moore's *Particulars of Place* (Omnidawn, 2105). Hillman teaches at St. Mary's College where she is the Filippi Professor of Poetry.

### Orb-Weaver Spiders, In Early Spring

Some of the new ones run past that
    left-leaning hill, but a few sleep here, the
    gray XX's & As from a rusted plan—; no war
with their species, no curve, no hand would
    interfere—; if only your nerves could be
    still for one minute! ceaselessly spelling over
your fresh grief with powdery letters, before
    dawn—; you see them with lines they
can't stop creating . . . A word has got
to join the slight staggering in the garden, to
    bring blue meaning, to the sleep of you—

---

## ALYSSA KELLY

Alyssa Kelly is a high-school English teacher, singer-songwriter, and poet. She has developed a year-long poetry curriculum aimed at engaging vocational students in the study and composition of verse, and she has twice served as the Teacher Fellow at the Frost Place in Franconia, New Hampshire. Her poetry has been published in *Uncommon Core*, a collection of contemporary poems meant for classroom use.

## Unforgivable

Most god-awful truth gets told when
it stir-crazies and sours like milk. When you
can't keep secrets quiet enough to even have
regrets. Most of Tuesday's mistakes are forgotten
by the time confessions cross their ankles Sunday
morning as polite little girls. Face it: we are halves
of love's whole, however clumsy our apologies appear in
flower vases, however our bodies measure distance in bed.

## MARCUS SEDGWICK

Marcus Sedgwick is the winner of many prizes, most notably the Printz Award
(Midwinterblood), the Booktrust Teenage Prize, and the Blue Peter Book
Award. His books have been shortlisted for over forty other awards, including
the Carnegie Medal (five times), the Edgar Allan Poe Award (twice), and the
Guardian Children's Fiction Prize (five times). In 2011 *Revolver* was awarded
a Printz Honor. He lives in the French Alps.

## Before That Sunday

That Sunday when you swore and
whipped my limping heart the most,
and expectation was undressed, especially,
that would be the moment when
you had forgotten me and I had forgotten you.
If you have, then say, I have,
And may I tell, that I have never forgotten
how gently we always flowed, always. Before that Sunday.

## LEONA SEVICK

Leona Sevick's work appears in the *Journal, Barrow Street, Potomac Review*
and the *North American Review*. She is the 2012 first-place winner of the Split
This Rock Poetry contest, judged by Naomi Shihab Nye. Her first chapbook,

*Damaged Little Creatures*, was published in 2015 by FutureCycle Press. She is associate provost and associate professor of English at Mount St. Mary's University.

## A Love Story

I want the fat, sniffling boy I'm eyeing in the public library to feel hugged,
though he doesn't know me and I wouldn't dare to touch him as I slip by.
Hunched over his paperback, upper teeth locking bottom lip firmly in place, my
new boy is a study in concentration, vertical lines separating plain,
upturned brows, a dignified jut to a jaw already looking old.
Brown eyes never leave the page while he folds his spent gum in a wrapper
and scans the lines for zombies, for robots or god-knows-what on this Sunday
    evening of
screaming sirens and faded yellow light. There is no such thing as no-expectation.

# XV

## DAN BEACHY-QUICK

Dan Beachy-Quick is a poet, essayist, and occasional novelist, whose most recent books include a study on John Keats, *A Brighter Word than Bright* (University of Iowa Press), and a book of poems, *gentlessness* (Tupelo). His work has been supported by the Lannan Foundation and the Guggenheim Foundation. He teaches in the MFA program in creative writing at Colorado State University.

### Places Never Gathered

Places never lived gather in the
artful child, desperate as toys
and those letters that in the desk are
open to no one's eyes. Nothing adds up to all.
In the eye's own cavern lives a monster, grotesque.
Serrate teeth are its least horror and
dangerous less than its voice which sings, "Not, not."
Are you a child?—these words are meant for
hands, so you must hold them lovely,
lovely, as you'd hold your mother's hands
for an hour in the doctor's waiting room. Are
not the silken flowers in the vase just as dangerous
and fatal as the real rose's serrate,
grotesque, petals and thorns? That monster in
all eyes names everything names open. Names open
are this monster's most dangerous song, "And, and." And
toys are just grown-up habits made artful:
the wise child is one who misplaces.

# You Did Not Know You Were Afrika

## WANG PING

Wang Ping has published eleven books of poetry and prose including *American Visa*, *Foreign Devil*, *Of Flesh and Spirit*, *New Generation*, *Aching for Beauty*, *The Magic Whip*, *The Last Communist Virgin*, and *10,000 Waves*. She's recipient of National Endowment for the Arts, Bush, Lannan, and McKnight fellowships. She's the founder and director of Kinship of Rivers project.

## She Shall Not Be

You order me to grow up and stop throwing "rage" around, and your
White secretary screams and scolds and sets up roadblocks for my work
Then reports them as proofs of my yellow chaos/incompetence so that
You Excellency can summon me to your palace to explain why I was
Such a challenge for everyone. But who's everyone and what have I done
Your Excellency, apart from making you stars with my blood? What evidence to
Back the charges you can't even name? Moxuyou—shadow daggers meant to be
Lodged in my organs . . . I was your Poster Babe, my art and teaching have done
You much glory, now I'm worse than a ghost—unseen, unheard, unspoken to
Only daggers of moxuyou . . . just because I said no . . . if this is your justice, let
    it be
A flower of truth . . . if this is your world of grown ups, then I'm done
With your rules of lies and hypocrisy. Let me sing in agony. To live is to
To fulfill the child's dream. Let her play and shake earth and sky. Let her be
Mother of conscience. You know she shall not be moved till the job is done.

------

Moxuyou: a Chinese term from the Song Dynasty (twelfth century), when the emperor charged and killed his general Yue Fei for treasons based on lies. *Moxuyou* became a synonym for groundless rumor, charges, persecution . . .

# Young Afrikans

## DEXTER L. BOOTH

Dexter L. Booth is the author of *Scratching the Ghost* (Graywolf Press, 2013), which won the 2012 Cave Canem Poetry Prize. Booth is included in *The Best American Poetry 2015,* and his poems appear in numerous publications. He is currently a PhD candidate at the University of Southern California.

### Neo-Afronaut Anthem

Told we are cursed, we sing hymns and
lift our tongues to the moon. Hoping they
hear us, we dance across this barque, await
the weightlessness of unruly being. Across
the universe we fly—in an oil drum or the
casing of a bullet—we outline the changes
we have made in history with chalk and
the shape is our bodies laid across the
doorstep of their god. Our future, spiraling,
free fall planet that it is, we will find it dead
if we cannot heave this slag. Believe me, our
fables don't end like this. We know the Black
because we come from it. The trope: revival
after three days in the dark. Records bay. Our
ancestors whir; strange fruit that grew black
on the rope's stemmed branches; *pour vinegar
on any wound: you'll find relief.* This is not our
science. Yesterday I drew a universe on my hands
and feet with the tip of a nail. I have chartered and
mapped this body so that it is safe to dream. Our
breath will form new constellations as we sing. Hot
and dense are our voices, hot and dense our blood.

---

## KIMIKO HAHN

Kimiko Hahn is author of nine collections of poetry, most recently *Brain Fever* (W. W. Norton) and five chapbooks of which she is very proud, including the forthcoming *Erasing Honor* (Phantom Limb) and *Resplendent Slug* (Ghost Bird). Hahn teaches in the MFA Program in Creative Writing and Literary Translation at Queens College, City University of New York.

## The Real Cool

The really cool ones figure as aunties, the
women who share their milkofhumankindness
in metaphor and Golden Rule. A must?
Hardly. And if shrill she can only be
evil stepmother, absent mom—not a Gwendolyn. Be mindful
of a shamaness who imparts as
"We Real Cool" imparts. Such a wily
classic, that woman! Toast with magnums of sparkling wines!

# Non-Brooks Golden Shovels

## HANA BEACHY-QUICK

Hana Beachy-Quick is a sixth-grader at Lesher Middle School in Fort Collins, Colorado.

### Golden Shovel

> *"My love—my love says*
> *she loves me.*
> *And that she would never have*
> *anyone but me."*
>
> *—Robert Creeley's "Stomping With Catullus"*

"Me" is not the same as "my,"
But why, love?
Anyone can say "my."
Have great fears, love,
Never face them. God says,
"Would you face them?" She—
She is one who loves
That you are mine with me,
And I am mine with you, and
Me is the same me that
Loves, she says. She—
She never would
Say never.
Love, I tell you, fears I have.
My love could be for anyone.
Love, I am. But
My "me" is not only me.

## CURTIS CRISLER

Curtis L. Crisler was born and raised in Gary, Indiana. He received a BA in English, with a minor in theatre, from Indiana University–Purdue University, Fort Wayne (IPFW), and he received an MFA from Southern Illinois University Carbondale. Crisler is an associate professor of English at IPFW.

> window blinds slice
> the sun into lemon pie wedges
> and then splatters them
> onto the wall
> Tuesday's divorce cramps
>
> —Antoinette Brim "mid-day"

On the other side of *that* window
to my soul, she always blinds—
the frowns in my heavy eyes—a slice
of wonder left like lone maple leaf on the
doorstep in the spring, where the sun
runs away from the rain, here, into
snatches of gray. There are no lemon-
yellow-things in bloom, or the smell of pie
slapping the nose to attention. It's the wedges
inside me she's compartmentalized, and
how those wedges weep. I must then
carry on with what happens to the splatters
a wedge can leave behind—the sticky of them
stepped upon—the residue of a body left onto
the naked foot, holding up all else in the
world. I tilt back on my only support—a wall.

## PHIL DACEY

Philip Dacey's latest book is *Church of the Adagio*; his previous, *Gimme Five*, won the 2012 Blue Light Press Award. He appears in *Scribner's Best American Poetry 2014*. Winner of three Pushcart Prizes, Dacey has published whole volumes of poems about Gerard Manley Hopkins, Thomas Eakins, and New York City.

## Parenthood

*Where my children are distances, horizons.*
                    —*Eavan Boland "the lost land"*

The journey must be near its finish. Where
Are my children? Where am I? How did all my
Steps lead nowhere? I can't see my children
Anywhere. Please say I am blind and they are
Next to me. No one spoke of distances
When I began, at a breast. I gave birth to horizons.

---

## KENDRA DECOLO

Kendra DeColo is the author of *Thieves in the Afterlife* (Saturnalia Books, 2014), selected by Yusef Komunyakaa for the 2013 Saturnalia Poetry Prize. She has received fellowships from the MacDowell Colony, Bread Loaf Writers' Conference, and is a visiting professor at Sarah Lawrence College. She lives in Nashville, Tennessee.

## Last Night On Earth We Go to Wendy's

*it is the creation of a quiet bright mind-space that allows for the deliciousness of genitalia to become obvious.*
                    —*Joe Wenderoth, "September 2, 1996"*

Starry-eyed and ravenous, we wait for it
to serenade us like a bullet singing to a wound. Is
this what you meant by romance? Me, scouring the
remains of my life over a pool of ketchup, thick as the blood of creation,
while the city blooms smoke, waiting to be swallowed? Out of
everything, I'll miss the oily contents of tin cans. Colored wrappers. A
fig eaten like a kiss in a stairwell. Your lips, potable wishes. The quiet
grace of Aphasia, the tranny cashier who sells us fish sandwiches, her bright
wand of a smile and galactic tits orbiting the fryer. I want to make mind-
love, she says now to the darkness. All this glittering space
and no foreplay. Is this what you meant by loneliness? That
stiff feeling in my hips like rust and rain, a surgery that allows

the patient to watch. We are waiting for
it with graffitied hearts, to discolor and gouge the walls of the
restroom where stains blossom into gesture, fingerprints, a deliciousness
hard-earned and wreaking, brought down from the heavens of
grease, and I'm glad for once to have a body with fingernails and genitalia,
a tongue like a squatter's den that knows every violet edge of evening, to
unfold syllables from the book of silences, where we become
gentle, sipping endless refills, and saying thank you, even when it's obvious.

---

## SHARON DOLIN

Sharon Dolin is the author of six books of poetry, most recently *Manual for Living* (University of Pittsburgh Press, 2016), *Whirlwind*, and *Burn and Dodge*, winner of the AWP Donald Hall Prize in Poetry. She directs the Center for Book Arts Annual Poetry Chapbook Competition as well as Writing about Art in Barcelona.

### It takes so little

*After W. C. Williams*

to breach these fixed margins so
you can reach beyond this much
too much condensery that depends
for its sustaining blue upon
belief in the stilled idea
of this water silo, this oak red
table, this browning wheat the wheel
of the sun turns into a barrow
-ful of grain—even these apples glazed
in the bowl still sweeten with
summer days of flame not just rain
though who doesn't pray for water
and a gyring figure beside
your own frame to upend the
static view that depends on white
specks you peck like feed for chickens

## NICK FLYNN

Nick Flynn has worked as a ship's captain, an electrician, and as a case worker with homeless adults. His most recent book is *My Feelings* (Graywolf Press, 2015), a collection of poems. His work has been translated into fifteen languages.

### Sky Burial

*After Lucille Clifton*

Vulture, follow me up: here is the arm
my mother held me aloft with (as

well as she could, until she couldn't), it
is cut free of her body now, pulled

away from her shoulder, away
from her breath, as you, Vulture, point

your wing toward her offered heart, toward me—
let's pound her fingers into paste, pound the hand

open, Come down, I chant, each word opens
the sky, the clouds need to be warned—once

she was hand & now she is wing, once she was dirt &
now she is air, she was food & now she is bird, she was

lifted & now she is gone.

## ANTHONY JOSEPH

Anthony Joseph is a Trinidad-born poet, novelist, musician, and lecturer. He is the author of four poetry collections; a novel, *The African Origins of UFOs;* as well as six critically acclaimed albums as a vocalist and poet. He lectures in poetry and creative writing at Birkbeck College, University of London.

*My wife with the back of a bird fleeing vertically*
                                        —*Andre Breton*

She threw verbs and arrows at my
skull till I broke like water in her peninsula, a wife
who breathing deep, murmurs, coy-like, with
the nape of a question for a neck. The more the
heat from the *galvanise* slapped back
and the red dirt blew up, I thought of
how hard she suffered on that gospel plough, w/out a
suffocating word, with the exact patience of a bird
in flight, piercing the web of time, fleeing.
I broke her back with an axe of sin. To be buried, vertically.

---

## IAN KHADAN

Ian Khadan is a poet, curator, editor, and performance coach who lives in New York City with his wife, brother, and dog.

### Death in Brain .

*After C. K. Williams*

moon glazed skin heels tar black hyacinth brain
lying on the bathroom floor the letting seeping in
through the cracks of tiles soaking drab red into his
fingernails here he is folded into himself and brain
it was a pleasant room before the habits of this old
man young too came to whisky souring his woman's
leaving he too leaving having sunken brain in his brain
salt on his lips and belly sucking the notes written on
his wrists reading like a milling of the brain milling of the
nights the obvious scamps in his plot boasting their filthy
triumph demon-hounded brain sprawled on the lovely floor
crawling like the crawling of corpses in caskets a swarm of
melancholy brain of Death Fugue brain sampling dark in his
unholy brain whisky caustic on tongue dark in his brain

## TONI ASANTE LIGHTFOOT

Toni Asante Lightfoot is native of Washington, DC, where she was president
of the African American Writer's Guild. She moved to Chicago and was the
director of writing programs at Young Chicago Authors. She currently consults
on curriculum development that integrates the arts and sciences. Lightfoot is also
studying acupuncture and herbology.

### Middle Dreams

*And with great fear I inhabit the middle of the night*
*What wrecks of the mind await me, what drugs*
*to dull the senses*

*                    —John Wieners "The Acts of Youth"*

Between real sleep and the waking spasm and
between what you are and what you with
the ignorant exuberance of youth thought a great
life would be, lay the between of hope and fear.

I am living a life I never knew possible for the "I"
of my youth to grow into. This body I inhabit
long ago betrayed me. By 22, it moved from the
smooth, taught, supple center to the broad middle

of a middle aged broad. I have had this body of
my middle age twice as long as I had the
great body glowing like morning, enticing night
with dance, bourbon, and "yes". Yesteryear is what

years of tomorrows have become. Wrecks
of relationships make the shoreline of
my memories fascinating. Among the
lost ships I visit when I have time for my mind

to salvage from them the shiny bits that await
my wiser translation of the loud, scared me

is the big hulking ship holding dreams. What
do I do to quell their haunting? Drugs,

whiskey? No, I line them up, look them over to
remind myself that I am "here" because "there" looked dull.
Under the magnifying glass of age the
bright light of perspective tantalizes my senses.

---

## BILLY LOMBARDO

Billy Lombardo is the author of *The Man with Two Arms, How to Hold a
Woman, Meanwhile Roxy Mourns*, and *The Logic of a Rose*. He teaches at the Latin
School of Chicago. Billy is a Nelson Algren Award winner and the founder and
managing editor of *Polyphony H.S.*, a student-run, international literary magazine
for high-school writers and editors.

### At Johnnie's after Basketball Practice

> *therefore their sons grow suicidally beautiful at the beginning of October and*
> *gallop terribly against each other's bodies*
> > —*James Wright "Autumn begins in Martins Ferry, Ohio"*

I have to remind myself to be reluctant therefore,
to leave the false calculus to planners—their
shames and their dreams like seeds in their sons.
Secret factors. They grow
them, their sons, in factories of plans. Live suicidally
for them, then sleep through all the beautiful
moments. Like that night after basketball at
Johnny's Beef. We had the radio on in the
Nissan that never belonged to us. We were beginning
the negotiation of dipped beefs and a new car and speaking of
math. It was only October
of your freshman year and I was already tired and
worried at your limping through algebra—your rage at the gallop-
ing greater thans—when you remembered, terribly,
about Kenny George and his halved foot. Against

the math and worry and Spanish and sleep—against each
of our rages, you woke me up to the sadness of others.
To the smallness, even of giants' bodies.

––––––––––

## NICK MAKOHA

Nick Makoha won the 2015 Brunel African Poetry prize and represented Uganda
at Poetry Parnassus as part of the Cultural Olympiad held in London, and his
one-man-show *My Father and Other Superheroes* is currently on tour. His poems
have appeared in *Poetry Review, Rialto, TriQuarterly Review,* and *Boston Review.*

## The Shepherd . . .

*At the violet hour, when the eyes and back*
*Turn upward from the desk, when the human engine waits*
*Like a taxi throbbing waiting,.*

—*T. S. Eliot "The Wasteland"*

. . . made no appeal. Spoke only of an assassination plot at
the diplomats' independence party. Caught whispers among the
bushes. Four men making finger-maps in the dirt. Dressed in violet
house-boy attire. Can you believe that at this hour?
Continue! Height: tall. Complexion: pallid, body hairs sheared. When
asked, he mimicked how each stood in formation. The
only time they relaxed was in the drawing of guns. In the eyes
an expansion. Continue! They were ready to die and
watch the world burn with them. Questioned for hours on his back.
His right cheek on the tarmac of a dual carriageway, a turn
of the neck to watch the stars with his flock. Their gaze upwards
interrupted by a blast of diesel and cough of smoke from
the right. A base hum tickling his shoulders rising through the
road. Two Coca-Cola soda crates were used as a makeshift desk
to the left. Continue! The voice from behind asked and when
the only answer was a sigh . . . (a meter was running) into the
evening. The voice took a blade. You'll always find a use for it. Humans
are pathetic. The voice asked another to dig some graves. Engine
off. This was not the shepherd's war, but yet he waits

and offers his body to those who beat him. Their faces and hands like
flint. In the first grave his feet, now just cuts of meat. A
second grave his arms dying like the rusty flowers by the taxi.
In the third and fourth, his cracked skull and torso throbbing.
The goats, searching for a command, grazing at his graves. Waiting!

————————

## BLAKE MORRISON

Blake Morrison is a poet, novelist, and the author of two bestselling memoirs,
*And When Did You Last See Your Father?* and *Things My Mother Never Told Me.*
He edited *The Penguin Book of Contemporary British Poetry* with Andrew Motion
and has published several collections of his own, the most recent of which is
*Shingle Street*, 2015. He is professor of creative writing at Goldsmiths College,
London.

### The Road to Wales

> *Life is first boredom, then fear.*
> *Whether or not you use it, it goes.*
>
> —*Philip Larkin "Dockery and Son"*

'You're old before you know it then—poof!—over, end of life.'
Dusk, the low sun blinding us, my dad at the wheel. Next week is
my tenth birthday and here we are going off together for the first
time. He flips down the sun visor. It's been all boredom
till now, a slow journey from Yorkshire to Wales. Then
the traffic clears and he puts his foot down. 'Death's nothing to fear,'
he says, overtaking a cattle-truck, 'It comes to us all.' Whether
they're meant to or not, his words fall like a shadow and I can't move or
speak. Of course I know everyone dies, but till now I've not
considered myself among them. 'Welsh border soon—when we
see a good pub, we'll stop. It'll be closing time soon and I could use
a pint.' He brings me half a shandy from the bar and I sip it
slowly, savouring the bitter new taste. 'We'll be there before you know it,'
he says, turning the key in the blackness of the car park. 'Here goes.

# JOHN O'CONNOR

John O'Connor is the author of *Rooting*, a chapbook of poems. His poems have appeared in places such as *Rhino; Cortland Review;* and *Poetry East.* He has also written two books of haiku and two books on teaching: *Wordplaygrounds* and *This Time It's Personal.*

## Immigrant

*After Carl Sandburg*

Most nights Dad'd be down
At The Six Penny Bit, wedged between
Shot glasses, a forest of flannel, and the
World's saddest jukebox, leaning against the back wall.
A small circle of
Followers mingling their shadows
Into his circle of darkness where
He'd sit like a *seanchai,* the
Tribal storyteller, with his rusty iron
Tongue, an illiterate man, expounding the laws
Of Immigrant Life, insist-
ing discrimination against the
Irish was different, that famine hunger
Was more hungry, the fist-thick brogues joining their voices
In agreement, their leader, haloed in cigarette glow, rising to mock-
Heroic exposulation. This was the only place where the man with the
Second grade education could ply these stories, as worn
As the grooves of the ancient 45s dropping on the juke box: another waif, airing
His grievances into a glass. How hard for the poor to live like men.
The night of his wake, I walked around the funeral home with
His Mass card in my hand. *Grant me the*
*Serenity to accept the things I cannot change . . .* hunched
Under the sodium-vapor streetlights he installed, and
Read the prayer he chose though he never learned to read. How humble
And frail he looked in the casket: "Big Mike" with the broad shoulders,
The man of smashed furniture-violence, who couldn't throw

Punches at the world, so he saved his anger for home, his wife and kids running
   for their
Lives, ducking the buckle of the work pants belt and the derisive laughter
Of neighbors. It's taken nearly 20 years for our stories to modulate into
Legend, our uneasy memories into tearless toil.

_____

## PASCALE PETIT

Pascale Petit's sixth collection *Fauverie* was shortlisted for the 2014 T. S. Eliot
Prize and won the Manchester Poetry Prize. Four of her books have been
shortlisted for the T. S. Eliot Prize and were chosen as Wales Books of the Year.
Bloodaxe Books will publish her next collection *Mama Amazonica* in 2017.

### Square de la Place Dupleix

*"Your family weaves you on devotion's loom, rick-racking the bed" from 'Cotton*
*Flannelette'*

—*Les Murray*

Inside the sandpit you are playing for your life. Your
bucket and spade that smiled all day long, like family
in your satchel, now work hard. Your material is sand. It weaves
a universe where you are huge, the cellar behind you,
eclipsed by twelve chestnut trees and their pigeon gods. On
and on you burrow, into your sanctuary, devotion's
priest. There are rituals to do, like counting leaves on the sky's loom.
Any lapse and you tumble back into the brain's forks, rick-racking
the minutes for the lock that unclicks, the coffining dark, the
hooded stranger with Papa's voice, the makeshift bed.

_____

## KEVIN SIMMONDS

Kevin Simmonds is the author of the poetry collections *Mad for Meat* and *Bend*
*to It* and the editor of *Collective Brightness: LGBTIQ Poets on Faith, Religion and*
*Spirituality* and *Ota Benga under My Mother's Roof.* He divides his time between
San Francisco and Japan.

## Social Security

*But the iron thing they carried, I will not carry.*
                                            —*Mary Oliver "Flare Poem"*

Soon momma's eligible but
it's much too late for boomers, the
long-uninsured with low iron,
bad gums, that diabetic thing
lodged long ago in the blood they
say is her own black fault, carried
from the womb since birthing me. I
can care for momma but what will
happen to those whose treasure's not
a child, only blood they carry?

---

## DOROTHEA SMARTT

Dorothea Smartt—"Brit-born Bajan international," live artist, and poet. *Connecting Medium* and *Ship Shape* are published with Peepal Tree Press. Her chapbook, *Reader, I Married Him . . .* (2014) is a "subversive" and life-affirming examination of "Black diasporic love." Her forthcoming collection, reworks hetero-normative narratives and imagines cross-gender experiences among "West Indians" constructing the Panama Canal.

## Headway

*down near the jetty where fishgutfunk fumed furiously*
                                    —*Anthony Joseph, African Origins of UFO*

The time was ripe to heal me. Lead me willingly down,
out past the lie, to our own brand of salvation. The near-
east, far-east, western, native American, the aboriginal, the
'Egyptian' paths to oneness, missing a voice. Out on the jetty
of my life so far, I'd had to wonder. I could see below, where
swirling swarms of hoodoo-voodoo priests, festish fishgutfunk
witch-doctors, obeah men, pocomania roots women fumed
at their muddied waters. In spite of lies making headway, furiously.

## LISA RUSS SPAAR

Lisa Russ Spaar is the author/editor of over ten books, including the forthcoming *Monticello in Mind: 50 Contemporary Poets on Jefferson and Orexia: Poems*. Her honors include a Rona Jaffe Award, a Guggenheim Fellowship, and the Library of Virginia Award for Poetry. She teaches at the University of Virginia.

### Even a Broken Clock Is Right Twice a Day

> *Squid-eyed Venus floats forth overhead*
> *—Charles Wright, "Body & Soul II"*

Last gray floe of spring snow in the brain, squid-
dim heaven, satellites failing, squint-eyed.
Where is the river, boatman of Venus,
the curious dog? What can't be told floats;
cut loose, expletive minutes issue forth:
the past—slingshot, pendulous—overhead.

## DAVID ST. JOHN

David St. John is the author of eleven collections of poetry (including *Study for the World's Body*, nominated for the National Book Award), most recently, *The Auroras* and *The Window*. He teaches in the PhD program in literature and creative writing at the University of Southern California.

### Robert Johnson's Double-Edged Shovel

> *I got to keep movin'*
> *Blues fallin' down like hail*
> *And the days keeps on worryin' me*
> *There's a hellhound on my trail*
> *—Robert Johnson*

I don't trust what I
Got & don't care what you got
To do I just know I got to
Keep it with mine so I'll keep
Movin' my blues by your movin'

Blues both our blues
Fallin' all over us like rain fallin'
Down your naked body down
Like little kisses like
Hail in our little hell

And every time I take your hand
The misery rises from the
Days I keep waking and this daze
Keeps on killing me keeps
On making me keep on
Worryin' the way you're worryin'
Me when you say to me
There's nothing left of us there's
A hole in the ground where a
Hellhound howls like a hellhound
On the scent of a body like the one
My soul gave up on as my
Trail blackened along my trail of trials

--------

## JEAN VALENTINE

Jean Valentine's thirteenth book is *Shirt in Heaven* (Copper Canyon Press, 2015).
In 1965 she won the Yale Younger Poets Award for her first book, *Dream Barker*,
and in 2004 she won the National Book Award for *Door in the Mountain: New
and Collected Poems*. She lives in New York City.

### Poem with Endwords by Reginald Shephard

> *there's never enough world for you*
> —*Reginald Shepherd " Occurrences across the Chromatic Scale"*

I saw it—there's
the bright snow—it's never
going to be enough
for this intimate world
—never intimate enough for
the 3rd strange angel, you.

## KAREN MCCARTHY WOOLF

Karen McCarthy Woolf holds a Glenna Luschei *Prairie Schooner* Prize and an Arts and Humanities Research Council doctoral scholarship at Royal Holloway, University of London, where she is researching new ways of writing about nature and the city. Her collection *An Aviary of Small Birds* is published by Oxford Carcanet.

## Of Ownership

*Take note of the proliferation of supermarkets and malls, the altars of money.*
*They best describe the detour from grace.*

—*Joy Harjo, "A Map to the Next World"*

The verb has a long history of violence: to take
is to grab, seize or capture, esp. by force; note
its hard 'k' set against the long vowel, a sign of
intent, this cave of sound. He took her by the
throat and shook her is one in a proliferation
of examples. To enter into possession or use of
(a thing) any thing, the things of supermarkets
that lull us as we push the trolley round and
round the soothing fountains in the malls,
always the polystyrene trays of flesh, bright in the
chilled, fluorescent aisles. Our Virgins at such altars
now are birds who've never felt the drum of
rain on their fattened breasts. Save money.
Buy one, get one free & variations thereon. They
(the shops) are here to help themselves as best
they can. Language is also ownership, we describe
our thoughts, precisely, and by default corral the
heart: most articulation is squandered as a detour
from love that manifests as pain inside us, from
what is felt, from the breath that connects us to grace.

## AVERY R. YOUNG

Multidisplinary artist avery r. young is a Cave Canem alum and 3Arts Awardee, whose work has appeared in *The BreakBeat Poets* and other anthologies. His recent release *booker t. soltreyne:a race rekkid* is a collection of sound design focusing on race, gender, and sexuality in America.

## pedagogy of a whoopin

*after Haki Madhubuti from Poet: Gwendolyn Brooks at 70*

cause rent money aint nothin to buy (penny)candy wif
& if him dont learn today him gonna find himself at de
gates wif bullet holes fo eyeballs merciful father let wind
& rhythm strike fire to dis herr switch & plant a seed in
him blkside so him may grow to understand dat yo
oven of thieves way mo scorchin den my good work hand

# Variation and Expansions on the Form

## RAPHAEL ALLISON

Raphael Allison's poems have appeared in *Tin House, Literary Review, Painted Bride Quarterly, Harvard Review,* and elsewhere. He is the author of *Bodies on the Line: Performance and the Sixties Poetry Reading.*

### Double Golden Shovel

*from kitchenette building*

We aren't much, we
are what we are

but sometimes less so, sucked threads from things
from which we weave ourselves, of

thicker cloths, costlier ones—dry
fabric, say, embroidered for hours

by hand, patiently, in a quiet room. And
then we're what's clipped off, cut, the

act of us is almost completely involuntary.
We were never too much a part of the plan.

We make, though, of what we
are given in stitches and samples

things no one could've bet on—unless
of course, one were a stitcher too,

dry-eyed and wary for so many
hours. It's not what we're handed, it's what we do

and how we needle
the twill that will,

involuntary as our own wishes,
plan our histories.

---

## JULIA ALVAREZ

Julia Alvarez is the author of numerous works of fiction, nonfiction, books for
children, and poetry (*Homecoming, The Other Side, The Woman I Kept to Myself*).
She is a writer in residence at Middlebury College and involved in a number of
literacy and advocacy projects in her native Dominican Republic.

### Behind the Scenes

*After you, Ms. Brooks*
*from behind the scenes*

You don't fool me pretending that you're gone, I
see you in the white margins even if you think
you're now invisible, even if you look like print to
everybody else. I'm in this line of work myself,
so I know how you've toiled to become the nobody somebody
reading doesn't see, as if the not-too stiffened stanzas got
ironed out, the sparkling rhymes buffed & put there
by themselves, and not because Nobody got there early

and was gone before the ink dried on her thumb. Early
on, I learned from reading your poems that there
are no shortcuts writing them, that each time I've got
to give up being the *VIP* Somebody,
get down on my weak knees, discard *myself,*
become the work we love. So here's to
you at the invisible controls, not gone as some think
but powerfully alive in poems swept clean of *I.*

## ELLEN BASS

Ellen Bass's most recent book is *Like a Beggar* from Copper Canyon Press. Her poetry has been published in *The New Yorker, American Poetry Review, New York Times Magazine,* and many other journals. She teaches in the MFA writing program at Pacific University. ellenbass.com.

### Morning (a twisted shovel)

*from Jesse Mitchell's Mother*

The morning of her death she
woke fierce, some dormant force revived,
insistent. For the last time
I sat my mother up, shifted the loose mass
of her body to lean against me. Her dried-up
legs dangled next to mine, a triumph
of will, all the mornings she forced
herself to spritz cheap perfume,
hoist each pendulous breast into
its halter, place the straps in the old
ruts. We were alone, petals
falling from bouquets crowded
around us. I pulled
some pillows behind me when I couldn't
hold her any longer
and we rested there, the
body of my mother slumped
against my breast, the slow droop
of green stalks in their vases.
Her long-exhaled breaths
kept coming against her
resolve. And in the exquisite
pauses in between
I could feel her settle—
the way an infant
grows heavier and heavier
in your arms
as it falls asleep.

## MELISA CAHNMANN-TAYLOR

Melisa "Misha" Cahnman-Taylor is professor of TESOL & World Language
Education at the University of Georgia and Beckman Award winner for
"Professors Who Inspire"; Fulbright Scholar in Oaxaca, Mexico; and winner
of three Dorothy Sargent Rosenberg Poetry Prizes, Her poetry book, *Imperfect
Tense* (Whitepoint Press), was published in 2016.

### Frijolero Ex-Pats

*from The Bean Eaters*

Pancita soup, tasajo,
chuletas de cerdo, they
search pocket dictionaries
for cuts of meat, eat

oxtail and tripe with pan casero
    (Oh! homemade!). Beans
baked in clay pots for days.
    "Gringos," sure, but mostly

they find the people kind,
    despite the "white" effect: this
means more costly taxi rides
    but also more respect. Old

people here treated with dignidad,
    the more grey or yellow,
the more Express their cards.
    This aging pair

in brand-new rugged pants,
    prance backpacked to dinner,
haggle rugs made by hand.
    "Casero?" Is

this the word? No: Hecho a mano.
    The price: absurd! A

gendered mistake (¿el mano?), verbs
    imperfectly tensed, their casual

errors make formal requests.
    Snowbirds in Mexico, no affair
for the fearful or frail. Pepto-bismol,
    probiotics, and plain

water in talavera, or in hand blown
    glass, flan on chipware
laced with lead. On Days of the Dead,
    why not dine on

green glazes? Free health care,
    cheap meds, a
doctor not needed, even
    Viagra pills in plain

white boxes at half their
    American price. And
playa resorts off season
    rejuvenate creaking

joints. They adapt backs
    to box springs of wood,
loom walls with fabric or
    ornaments pressed from tin,

all lightweight,
    then packed flat
    into bags checked to where
they March home.

## MARILYN CHIN

Marilyn Chin is an award-winning poet. Her poems are considered Asian American classics and are taught all over the world. She has published five books of poems, including *Hard Love Province; Rhapsody in Plain Yellow; The Phoenix Gone, the Terrace Empty;* and a book of fiction called *Revenge of the Mooncake Vixen.* She lives in San Diego.

### Sadie and Maud, Redux

*from Sadie and Maud*

Maude says: Oh sad and stupid Sadie
You're a cliché ghetto bore!
Supporting not just one loser boyfriend, but two
And a litter of hell-bound babies.

Oh wretched lonely Maud! replies Sadie.
You're an uppity old maid bore!
Too ugly to keep a two-
Legged man, so you hoard stray cats like babies.

Dear dear stupid Sadie!
Dear dear wretched Maud!
Are you the truth or a cliché, dear Sadie.
Are you a cautionary tale, dear Maud.

## FRED D'AGUIAR

Fred D'Aguiar is a poet, novelist, and playwright. He teaches creative writing at University of California, Los Angeles.

### Golden Shovel Borrowed from Derek Walcott and Gwendolyn Brooks

In that ragbag Calypso down in Trinidad
The braggadocio of the frontloaded word, bad,
For how good steel drums shaped for pan sound
With a Spock-like ear to the wok-burnt ground.

A manual, as yet unwritten, begs all who celebrate
To step, dip and throw hips from side to side,
Arms stretched for balance as if testifying, and breathe,
Oh sweaty body caught in rapture with nothing to hide.

But who will feed the hungry as they choke down weed
To suppress a hunger that cannot be assuaged?
I ask as I lift a gilded flask, throw back my head,
Swallow over-proof rum to add backbone to this page.

In the field beside the residence of the President
There's a serious football match (soccer to you),
The boys in red take on the boys in blue in a recent
Signed peace. I send this from my I-pad, in a stew,

In a funk, for this is not the usual me; not the me,
Of me and you; but of enema, over hunger; of enemy,
Over anger; of no socks left to pull up, hangover;
In a blame game of Wikipedia fame; jilted lover.

---

## CALVIN FORBES

Calvin Forbes teaches classes in literature, creative writing, and jazz history at the School of the Art Institute of Chicago. He is the author of *Blue Monday* and *The Shine Poems* and has received grants and fellowships from the National Endowment for the Arts, the Illinois Arts Commission, and the Washington D.C. Commission on the Arts and has been a Fulbright fellow teaching at the University of Copenhagen, Denmark.

### The Devil's Own

*from a song in the front yard*

I've been bad all my life
Been left way out back
Ignored like a weed grows.
I am definitely not a rose.

I'm in the back yard now
Just down the alley.
Please come out and play.
I promise you a good time today.

We will do lots of fun things.
And have us some big fun.
Forget your mother's house is fine.
Nobody will be home until after nine.

Though your name isn't Mae
Or Bess girl you're now a woman.
Oh please baby don't be late—
Don't forget to lock the back gate.

I won't love you unless you say I do.
You want to be a bad woman too
Who confuses nylon with lace—
Come out here and say that to my face!

————

## DAVID GILMER

David Gilmer is a high-school English teacher in Chicago.

### When a Grief Has Come

*For A. J. Mayo*
*from "still do I keep my look, my identity . . ."*

What can I get you? Coffee, pop, or
maybe some water? Push
off your shoes. Be still. Of
course this is yours now. No pain
here child, no worries here. Sit still—
be calm. Can I cook some dinner? Or
maybe a nap? Trip long? When
you wake up this will not be a dream. A

calm eventually comes and then grief.
But even grief will pass. This place has
that effect. Let peace be stabbed,
through and through, be bled out. Or
maybe we will let tissue. Hatred
can be a snot filled hanky. Hacked
up lungs and red eyed eyes wet still—

What I mean to say is
welcome home its
not much to look at and
really its nothing
much, but it's ours and no one else's.
Take comfort that as each
day passes the images of his body
to will fade. Till nothing's left. Has
it been three days or three months? Its
time to let him go. Time to forget his pose.

*after Patricia Smith*

## KEITH JARRETT

Keith Jarrett writes poetry and short fiction and has taught as part of a
pioneering Spoken Word Educator program in London. A former United
Kingdom poetry-slam champion and Rio International Poetry Slam winner,
he is now a PhD scholar at Birkbeck University of London, completing his
first novel.

## Outside St. Dominic's Priory. Snapshot, July 2015.

*from Beverly Hills, Chicago*

From my neighbour's jaw-stretch gentrification monologue, I surmise: They
—men—are ignorant of the cost of a weave-on, while they—women—make
no effort to know the price of a night bus; and only *they*—children—excellent
students of their own self-worth, *do* know the value of their lives. Two corpses,

one called *Brother* and *Son* (again, I surmise) bottleneck my road, stuck among the school-run traffic. A sharp voice conducts a maroon Volvo's U-turn from the fifth floor. My phone dings. *Rebecca added #alllivesmatter.* They're expensive them phones, he quips. I bite my tongue and inhale black fumes, funeral flowers . . .

**

*My only defense is the present tense.*

Trigger warning: Because this is the poem where a lion dies. My better judgement requires me to name him. In this climate, only *Cecil, Mufasa* or *Aslan* will do. Under any other alias, the defense council will argue the officer felt *under threat.* So now my finger is swiping away the same comment: *Where is our Straight Pride* the man posts, *our White History Month?* Mindfulness: remain present and breathe; keep upright; shake vigorously. His paws, still tense.

**

Footnotes.

I remember, somehow, it began like this: *One night I was walking along the beach . . .* (it concluded, I think with one set of footnotes in the poem* . . . *Because it was then that I carried you*). Swallow the salt, † it must bring out the sweet, you said. I am lost. I count. To be alive, just this one body; perhaps, six uncracked lonely eggs; seven pairs of angry shoes, shuffling for space to be noticed. A clock, infinitely unforgiving. I want to be the second dent in this bed, instead of its single God.

---

*"It" here is deliberately obtuse, referring either to a dream, creation itself or the last moments of a relationship.

---

†Here the author is drawn to the body of Lot's wife, changed into salt for turning back. Here the author meditates on seasoned, almighty wrath, visiting those who hesitate, those who glance at what they leave behind.

## A. VAN JORDAN

A. Van Jordan is the author of four collections: *Rise, M-A-C-N-O-L-I-A,
Quantum Lyrics,* and *The Cineaste.* Jordan has been awarded a Whiting
Writers Award, an Anisfield-Wolf Book Award, and a Pushcart Prize. He is
a recipient of a John Simon Guggenheim Fellowship and a United States
Artists Fellowship. He is the Henry Rutgers Presidential Professor at Rutgers
University–Newark.

### People Who Have No Children Can Be Hard

*from The Children of the Poor*

And our nights wear on, not knowing who our people
will be to carry on, not so much in our name, but who
will benefit from the work of this life. Those who have
given birth or just said, *We're pregnant,* as a man—no
substitute: Once they worry over the fevers of their children,
they say, no other worries loom as large. Every bill can
be paid; the house's creaks can be fixed. What can't be
can be forgotten. But living without a child's cry? That's hard.

Then there are days when living alone isn't so hard,
at all. I learn to create the world I hope to be
in and why not? My friends complain: *We can't
go to the movies, on a hot date, can't getaway without this child.*
When I hear their gripes, I feel like I already know
what's behind the curtains of their eyes; promises have
been made and regretted. And then I feel lucky, *He who
lives the life!* I say—knowing I'd trade dates for diapers any day people.

## AMIT MAJMUDAR

Amit Majmudar is a poet, novelist, and essayist whose work appears widely. His
latest collection of poetry is *Dothead* (Alfred A. Knopf, 2016).

## Selected Psalms from the Book of Brooks

*from "still do I keep my looks, my identity . . ."*

*1. tired power a culprit wearing dirty ribbons*

Done running, Lord. Done now. Tired.
Overtake and overpower

this fugitive. Exhibit A:
My soles. Law, call me your culprit,

only call me yours. I'm wearing
flesh that's stained human, Lord, dirty

flesh. Here, Lord. Cut me to ribbons.


*2. our Black revival, our Black vinegar,*

No light, Lord, no more White light. Our
eyes need Black now. Knock-out-punch Black.

Black leather Bible revival.
Pepper and ink, not the salt of our

Sweat. Black Label, Lord, mixed with Black
Coffee. Hold the White vinegar.

---

## CAROL MUSKE-DUKES

Carol Muske-Dukes is author of eight books of poems, four novels, two
collections of essays, and has co-edited anthologies. She is a professor of English/
creative writing at the University of Southern California. She publishes widely
and is the recipient of many awards, including a Guggenheim, and National
Endowment for the Arts. www.carolmuskedukes.com.

## Accident

*from Jesse Mitchell's Mother*

Bad synapse: last hope, this idea
the lost might be saved! Nope. Dice
roll. That magician with the accent
keeps flashing spades: deuces & aces.
Silent cries hover above a calendar date
circled again & again: those Ides
of Fate, revisited. But you can't
make luck happen this late. You tend
to keep thinking backwards, indent
the ending in your mind. Let the moving tide
reveal what remains. Or what, like a habit, re-dies.

---

## MOLLY PEACOCK

Molly Peacock is the author of six books of poetry, including *The Second
Blush* and *Cornucopia* (W. W. Norton and Company). She is also the author
of *Alphabetique: 26 Characteristic Fictions,* illustrations by Kara Kosaka, and
*The Paper Garden: Mrs. Delany Begins Her Life's Work at 72* (Bloomsbury).
She serves as series editor of *The Best Canadian Poetry.*

## The Art of the Stroke:

*from "still do I keep my look, my identity . . ."*

Each body has its art. All parts of you, each
artery and vein of your brain, make a body,
and if part of it explodes, your soul still has
a place in the rest, doesn't it? Doesn't its
essence still speak, still practice its art
even when you can't fill a sentence with its
words? You still eat with gusto! That's a precious
urge from your hand to your tongue, desire prescribed.
Isn't there a special yoga pose

of Spoon-in-Hand? Though your living wills oppose
the state you're in, your specialist prescribed
acute rehab. All you claimed as precious
surfaced in a single sentence that forced its
meaning, Let me die, to create an ending art
with the soul—that's what's left, isn't it?—as sculptor of its
ragged material. And when the soul has
finished the work of its clay heart, clay brain, clay body
each spark can misfire and each body part, each . . .

———————

## TOM SLEIGH

Tom Sleigh's books include *Station Zed*, *Army Cats* (John Updike Award from the
American Academy of Arts and Letters) and *Space Walk* (Kingsley Tufts Award).
He's received the Poetry Society of America's Shelley Prize, a Guggenheim grant
and two National Endowment for the Arts grants, and many others. He teaches
at Hunter College and does journalism in the Middle East and Africa.

### Net

*from The Children of the Poor*

1.

It was said to be terrible, her temper,

but even more terrible was how she lost it—I mean lost it in the
    sense that trees

lose leaves, in that after she lay down on the table and they gave her
    electroshock, her anger simply fell away from her: it was like
    watching something or someone musical

go hopelessly, and forever, out of tune. For the other side of her
    disease,

the passivity, the compassionating hopelessness that afflicted her
　　　whenever her rage fell away, now took over—and she saw all
　　　too clearly her exposure high on the cliffs to the hungry beaks
　　　that in her lack of anger, she could no longer beat back
　　　as they swooped down to peck and eat.

Of course none of this happened inside the analytical logics of my
　　　sentences, both too precise and not precise

enough: the flat affect and opacity of her eyes

turned her into a stranger standing just outside the asylum
　　　doorway, staring at children on the lawn on a visiting Sunday
　　　who kept swinging badminton rackets at a birdie, playing
　　　without a net because they'd been told by other children that
　　　the patients weren't allowed nets because they'd try to steal
　　　them and use them as ladders to escape from their windows or
　　　worse, try to hang themselves—so she stands here, and also
　　　there, in my sentences that I know didn't know, and still don't
　　　know enough

about her to say what her rage, all these years later, might mean.
　　　What do the children know about how hard it is to play
　　　without a net? Do they even notice how the harder the rackets
　　　hit, the higher and more gracefully the birdie floats until it
　　　soars above the net that isn't there and, up among the trees,
　　　gets lost in falling leaves?

2.

　　　　　　　　　　　　When she calls me today, only
minutes ago, to tell me the unalloyed stuff

of her dream, she's riding on what she calls "that hot-bottomed bus,
　　　when we were all coming home, and there were chickens flying
　　　around the bus, and a little pig in a wooden cage in the aisle,
　　　and when we stopped I said to a man, *Where are we?* and he

said in perfect English, *In Mexico*, and there were a lot of
tourist shops," she said, "and so I got off the bus to look, and
there was a balloon man selling helium balloons," and she
said, "Oh Tom, the balloons were all so colorful, and there
was one of a cow, a bright yellow cow, and I wanted that one
so badly, such a beautiful cow, and when I looked around, the
bus was gone

and I was left alone

but there were hundreds of yellow cows all floating above the
    street."

---

## JACINDA TOWNSEND

Jacinda Townsend is the author of *Saint Monkey* (Norton, 2014), which is set in
1950s eastern Kentucky and won the James Fenimore Cooper Prize for historical
fiction.

### Father

*After Rhianna Gides*
*from My Little 'Bout-town Gal*

The father of the bride, a failed detective
sat at home on his daughter's wedding day, knitting his aging fingers
wondering about the world of
tolerant people. And why the sun shone on the mess of
this, his worst day. And why nothing had stayed as it was when Sputnik
launched, and why salt couldn't stay salt, and why pepper could not
stay pepper, and why no one but him understood that the two
should never mix. And why seasons change, and dirt becomes
mud, and simply why anything was anything at all. And whether the
skin of his Black daughter would shine white later, under the moon.

## CATHERINE WAGNER

Catherine Wagner is the author of four books of poems, most recently *Nervous Device* (City Lights, 2012). She directs the MA/MFA/BA program in creative writing at Miami University, Ohio.

### A Chat with the Endwords

*from Appendix to the Anniad*

*Sympathy says*: I like to watch. I need to watch.

*See says*: I like to be noticed, Sympathy, but your hospital scent is vague.

*Well needs*: Clean water, companions, exercise, nutrients, and on the job, a lithe and gummy vagueness.

*Charm advises*: Pucker the social seam and hide decay.

*Discreet suggests*: Ignore or plausibly deny my corpse, community watch.

*Property claims*: You're unwelcome to my world and its onus smell.

*Sweetness cries*: The world is rich, and oh, my livers, much wine is sweet.

*Smell says*: I'm sniff, minus intention. I happen undefiant as you breathe.

*Watch ticks a box*: Remains, discreet.

*Decay casts*: A zombie charm.

*Vagueness shares*: Deepwater Horizon well, Marcellus Shale well, all's well.

*Watch, seconding Vagueness*: You look better when I take my contacts out, see.

## BUDDY WAKEFIELD

Buddy Wakefield, from Los Angeles, California, by way of Boulder, Colorado, by way of Seattle, Washington, by way of Baytown, Texas, by way of Sanborn, New York, by way of Shreveport, Louisiana, is a three-time Poetry Slam world champion by accident. He likes peanut butter, Vipassana, cheering for exhausted runners and currently studies propellers because they can make themselves invisible.

### A Private Service Announcement

*from "Truth tellers are not always palatable", a Gwendolyn Brooks quote*

We could stick wet graph paper perfectly to the inner circle of a crooked truth hinged on bilateral balloon animal pyramids built by fortune tellers

while square dancing under a mobile of linear plains upon which there are
rows of microscopes angled above amoebas in subatomic cookie cutters not
subject to the laws of a time frame, centered between disconnected dots, always
symmetrically fluidly streaming, and still not shape a view that is, to you, palatable.

---

## TYRONE WILLIAMS

Tyrone Williams is the author of five books of poetry, *c.c.* (Krupskaya Books,
2002), *On Spec* (Omnidawn Publishing, 2008), *The Hero Project of the Century*
(Backwaters Press, 2009), *Adventures of Pi* (Dos Madres Press, 2011), and *Howell*
(Atelos Books, 2011). He is also the author of a prose eulogy, *Pink Tie* (Hooke
Press, 2011). His website is at http://home.earthlink.net/~suspend/.

## That's Mr. Robert Johnson to You

*from my dreams, my works, must wait till after hell*

I front. Twang
bid. Float they.
Be bee. And
firm fingered, I
till frets, incline
I strum this
return ear to ear
from heaven sent to
hell. Bent tin.

# *Afterword*

A century after her birth, Gwendolyn Brooks remains a pioneer; hopefully this anthology has sent you back to her magisterial work, not just to the widely anthologized poems, but to those poems you might not have encountered before. This collection testifies to her influence, still strong among contemporary writers, and to the invention of a brand new form, the Golden Shovel, something which we imagine Ms. Brooks would heartily approve. For as she herself has written, "very early in life I became fascinated with the wonders language can achieve. And [then] I began playing with words."

Whether you are a teacher or a student, a practicing or aspiring poet, a reader or a writer, a critic or someone who just likes to play with words, we offer you the Golden Shovel to put alongside those sonnets, villanelles, and sestinas of yesteryear. As you can see from the range of work we've included here, the potential applications of this form are vast, and there's a special kind of excitement that comes from charging language so that it can convey meaning in multiple ways, from hiding words so that a poem can contain a secret interior meaning. We hope that you will be inspired to take the Golden Shovel and dig with it yourself—experimenting with the form, teaching it to students of all ages, using it as a platform to delve more deeply into the literary and cultural history of your own country, and ultimately reveling in the pleasures of language.

To end, we'd like to leave you with some quotes from some of our Golden Shovel poets who've also discovered the joys of Ms. Brooks and using this new form, which we hope you find as addictive and gratifying as they have. The editors and University of Arkansas Press would be glad to hear about your own responses to using this new form and in the meantime, may all your digging be golden!

"This is a rather lovely way of working."

—George Szirtes

"Thanks for inviting me to take part in this adventure."

—Jean Valentine

"Wow-the stricture enforced a letting go! I imagine I'll write more of these. Thanks for inviting me to participate and introducing me to this form."

—Ellen Doré Watson

"It's been a real pleasure working on this poem. . . . It's also been great to really spend time with Brooks. I'd only known her in the most fragmentary way,. and feeling the full impact of her brilliance has been a gift. I also wanted to share with you that my 7-year old daughter and I have been working on some of these together. She picks up a book from the shelf, picks a line or two, and we write one together. They've come out quite strange and beautiful. . . ."

—Dan Beachy-Quick

"Well, you inspired me to try my hand at one of these. I really enjoyed the experience, and it gave me an idea for what could develop into an interesting series, so thank you for that!"

—Ronald Wallace

"An irresistible invitation. I'll try and have something for you before the end of March. [Then, a couple of hours later.] In fact, so irresistible that i could not go to bed before writing this."

—Alicia Ostriker

# Title Index

# Author Index